IN PRAISE C
YOUR BUSINESS YOU

The sage advice in these pages are worth their weight in gold to any small business. the only accountant that made me feel okay around the books, numbers and accounts for my business. Better understanding really does lead to better decisions and a better run business.

David Hyner of Stretch Development Limited
professional goal setting researcher and motivational speaker

This is a really practical and insightful book from someone that knows business, accounting and people! A must read for anyone starting out or in a business that they want to grow.

Adrianne Carter of D-Coded Insights Limited

As in her other books, Anna takes a daunting business challenge and breaks it down into easily digestible and manageable chunks. Her accessible approach and jargon-free language is a welcome breath of fresh air and makes the topics she covers relatable and understandable. Her chapter on 'Setting your goals' confidently mentors from initial business idea to 5-year objectives - valuable for would-be entrepreneurs just starting out to established business owners needing new inspiration.

Suki K Bassi
Chief Happiness Officer of Bishan Uttam Consulting Limited

It's a great read – accessible, plain language providing useful guidance and tips in a clear and structured approach, equipping the reader with the tools to apply the thinking. A valuable resource to anyone, not just those in business.

Elaine Woodman | Learning and Development Manager | whg

I've read a lot of business books in my time, but this one really stands out from the crowd. Not only is it crammed full of solid advice, it is a workbook too, allowing you to see how your own numbers stack up. A must-read for all small business owners!

Philip Oakley, Xero Technologist

After reading chapter 3 of Anna's latest book I feel much more aware of time management and it has left me feeling better able to tackle this longstanding challenge I have. The tips section is great and the way that it has been laid out really makes it much easier to digest and make real use of it rather than like many books, reading it and not implementing the new changes and ideas. My favourite part has to be the last section of the chapter where you can write down your actions to start making use of the knowledge Anna has gained from her own experiences. The diagrams and bullet points make it easy to digest what you need to know and in turn helping you remember the importance of time management when running a business. I will definitely be buying the book and look forward to implementing new habits into the daily running of my business. Thank you Anna.

Susan Prosser, Holistic therapist

*Dedicated to Mark Gooding. I learnt a lot from you.
Thank you.*

YOUR BUSINESS YOUR NUMBERS

ANNA GOODWIN

Your Business Your Numbers
A practical guide to small business success

Copyright © 2018 Anna Goodwin

www.annagoodwinaccountancy.co.uk

The moral rights of Anna Goodwin to be identified as the author of this work have been asserted in accordance with the Copyright, Designs and Patents Act 1988.

Copyeditor and Proofreader: Siân-Elin Flint-Freel

Design and typesetting: Tanya Bäck (www.tanyabackdesigns.com)

Illustrator: Lucy Monkman

All rights reserved. No part of this publication may be reproduced, stored in a retrieval system, or transmitted in any form or by any means, electronic, mechanical, photocopying, recording or otherwise, without the prior written permission of the copyright owner.

First published in 2018 by Anna Goodwin

ISBN 978-0-9930166-4-6

All the information, concepts, skills, techniques and any advice contained within this publication are of general comment only and are not intended in any way for any individual. They are the views and impressions of the author only. The intent is to offer a variety of information and circumstances to provide a wider range of choices now and in the future, recognising that we all have widely diverse circumstances and viewpoints. While all attempts have been made to verify information provided in this publication, neither the author nor the publisher nor the marketing agents assumes any responsibility for errors, omissions or contrary interpretation of the subject matter whatsoever under any condition or circumstances. Should any reader choose to make use of the information contained herein, this is their decision and the author and publisher do not assume any responsibility. It is recommended that the reader obtain their own independent advice.

YOUR BUSINESS YOUR NUMBERS

A PRACTICAL GUIDE TO SMALL BUSINESS SUCCESS

ANNA GOODWIN

CONTENTS

Introduction 7

Chapter 1: It's All About You 9

Chapter 2: Setting Your Goals 17

Chapter 3: Organising Your Time 27

Chapter 4: Knowing Your Numbers 33

Chapter 5: Understanding Your Accounts 49

Chapter 6: Pricing Your Way To Business Success 61

Chapter 7: Budgeting For Your Success 73

Chapter 8: Managing Your Business 81

Chapter 9: Mastering Your Personal Finances 95

Over to You 107

INTRODUCTION

You may have just set up in business or you may have been running your business for a while. But you may feel stuck:

- You know you have goals to set but you don't know where to start.

- You can't understand how time runs away with you.

- Your profit margins are low but you're not sure how to do anything about it.

- You're worried about Making Tax Digital but you don't know which software package to choose.

And plenty more…

There are loads of books which tell you how to run your business and how to sort out your accounts. Why is this book different? Yes, there are things you need to do in a certain way but how *you* run *your* business can be done *your* way. You have the choice and this book will give you the courage to do it your way.

If you're left handed you wouldn't force yourself to write right handed. So, don't do this in your business either! Do it your way and I'm here to guide you through it.

CHAPTER 1

IT'S ALL ABOUT YOU

"Knowing yourself is the beginning of all wisdom."
– Aristotle

In order to be successful in business, you need to know yourself. Whether or not you're just setting up in business of if you've been running your business for a few years it's always good to know your strengths, weaknesses, passions and your preferred way of working.

Many of us start off more by accident than design, which is fine, but as your business develops you can reflect on your character and begin to plan for the future. The more you know yourself the more you might want to change the way you work.

By having a better understanding of yourself you will know which parts of the business you should lead, where you can delegate, and when you work best in the day. This will all increase your chances of making your business a success.

WHO ARE YOU?

Give yourself some time to think about you as a person: what you like doing and what you dislike doing, as well as your personality traits. These questions will help you to move your business forward as you will understand the best way for you to work.

- What are your strengths and weaknesses?
- Are you a patient person?
- Are you an ideas person?
- Are you an instinctive person?
- Are you risk averse or happy to take risks?
- Do you thrive on a challenge or would you rather take it steady?
- Have you had lots of different jobs and gained a lot of knowledge about different industries or have you stayed in one job?

WHO ARE YOU?

WHAT DO YOU BRING TO YOUR BUSINESS?

This is important to consider at every stage in your business — not just when you start up. Your circumstances could have changed in the last 12 months so it is always worthwhile to review what you can bring to your business.
- Do you have capital to invest? e.g. do you have savings or money from family or friends, or maybe you are eligible for a grant?
- Do you have the relevant qualifications? Will you need specific training?
- Is your previous experience relevant to what you will be doing now?

WHAT DO YOU BRING TO YOUR BUSINESS?

HOW DO YOU LEARN?

- Listening to an audio recording?
- Watching a video on YouTube?
- Attending a lecture?
- Attending a webinar?
- One-to-one mentoring?

If you have said that you prefer to learn through one-to-one mentoring and you always give up half way through a video tutorial, then it is not worth wasting your time subscribing to lots of online training by video. You just won't complete it and will beat yourself up. However, you may like attending lectures as it is the personal approach you prefer. On the other hand, if you dislike interacting with people face to face (though I am sure you have to do it at some point in your business!), then you may find webinars, videos and audio recordings the best way to learn.

All I ask of you is to have a good think about *what* and *how* you learn from your preferred methods. What do you take away from them? How do you use what you have learned? There is no point sitting through countless video tutorials, wasting hours of your time, if you don't action anything after watching it! On the other end of the scale, maybe you don't partake in any learning or training. This is a mistake! You always have to keep on top of what is new in business in general and in your particular field. Maybe ease yourself in gently by booking on a short webinar or face-to-face tutorial.

HOW DO YOU LEARN BEST?

HOW DO YOU WORK?

- Are you happy working on your own or do you prefer working as part of a team?
- Are you a last-minute kind of person or would you prefer to get things done early?
- Are you happy with using technology?
- Are you happy working alone or do you need other people around you?
- At what time of day do you work best?
- Where do you like to work? On your own or in an area with others?
- Are you happy to delegate or do you feel that you need to be involved in everything at every stage?

Work to your strengths, e.g. if you work better in the morning when you are fresh, set aside time then to do your main work that needs a lot of thought. Perhaps you could keep your mundane admin tasks for the afternoon. Are you an owl or a lark? Would you be able to work from home on your own for most of the day? These are all things to consider when setting up in business. However, even if you have already established your business, you can always review the way you work to see if what you have set up works for you. Perhaps you have been working in a home office for a while and you are finding it a lonely experience. Why not consider using a communal office space a couple of times a week or build a team around you?

HOW DO YOU WORK?

YOUR BUSINESS STRUCTURE

This is an important consideration, whether you are an existing business or just starting up. There will be different aspects to think about and different ways of working depending on your structure. Each structure will have different deadlines, tax implications, and ways of withdrawing money from the business, so it is worth taking some time to research each structure and how it will impact on you.

For example, a disadvantage of being a sole trader would be having full liability if the business fails. An advantage would be that the structure of a sole trader is easier to understand. An advantage of a limited company is being able to pay yourself in dividends. A disadvantage would be having to understand the way it works.

These are the most common structures but you may decide the other structures are a better fit for you. Even if you already have a business, you may want to review your business structure to see if it is still fit for purpose. Possibly you set it up as a sole trader as it was easier and yet now is the time to become a limited company.

If I was a:	This would be the impact on me or n/a:
Sole trader	
Limited company	
Partnership	
Limited liability partnership (LLP)	
Charity	
Community interest group (CIC)	

YOUR BUSINESS

> *"There is no substitute for accurate knowledge.
> Know yourself, know your business…"*
> *- Lee Iacocca*

In order to be successful, you not only need to understand yourself but also your business — in its entirety. Even when you subcontract or delegate, you always need an overview of every aspect of the business and you need to understand it — no more so than when you are talking about your finances, which we will return to later in the book.

- What are your main products/services?
- Who are your competitors? Do you have one main one or several?
- Who are your ideal customers? Spend some time considering this, being as detailed and specific as possible.
- What industry are you in? How do you keep updated on any advances in your industry?
- Do you have any employees? If so, are you up to date with auto enrolment, HR etc.
- Are you VAT registered or near the VAT limit so this will soon be a consideration?
- What expenses are allowable for your business? Are you happy that you know this or do you need to check this with your accountant?

Think about the questions and write down your answers. If you don't know the answers, how are you going to find them?

It is important to take ownership of your business and know that its success relies on you.

Here are some more questions for you to answer to help you to know yourself better and therefore be more successful with your business, before we begin to be more specific about what you want to achieve with your business.

Question	Action
What are your 3 biggest business challenges?	1. 2. 3.
What are your 3 biggest strengths?	1. 2. 3.
What are your 3 biggest successes in life? *This can be in your home or business life.* *This highlights the areas where you excel and also motivates you to succeed.*	1. 2. 3.
What has held you back in your life and what did you learn from these experiences?	1. 2. 3.

CHAPTER 2

SETTING YOUR GOALS

"Setting goals is the first step in turning the invisible into the visible."
- Tony Robbins

Have you thought about where you want your business to be in five years' time? Are you clear about what your main objective is at the moment? Do you know what you are working towards?

So now you are clearer about who you are, your strengths and the structure of your business to suit you, you can begin to focus on your goals.

If you want to succeed, you need to set goals. Without goals you lack focus and direction. Goal setting not only allows you to take control of your business's direction, it also highlights whether you are succeeding.

WHY ARE GOALS IMPORTANT?

As Alice says to the Cheshire Cat in Lewis Carroll's Alice's Adventures in Wonderland:

> *"'Would you tell me, please, which way I ought to go from here?'*
> *'That depends a good deal on where you want to get to,' said the Cat.*
> *'I don't much care where,' said Alice.*
> *'Then it doesn't matter which way you go,' said the Cat."*
> *- Lewis Carroll*

So, if you do care about which direction you're going, set goals.

Goals:
- Provide focus.
- Give us the ability to set the exact actions we need to complete to achieve everything we desire in life.
- Cause us to stretch and grow.
- Provide long-term vision in our lives to help us get past any short-term obstacles.

"Successful people maintain a positive focus in life no matter what is going on around them. They stay focused on their past successes rather than their past failures, and on the next action steps they need to take to get them closer to the fulfilment of their goals rather than all the other distractions that life presents to them."
- Jack Canfield

WHAT DO YOU WANT FROM YOUR BUSINESS?

Think about what you want from your business. In order to reach your goals, you need to follow specific steps for this to happen. Unfortunately, you can't just wave a magic wand!

To decide what you want, it's important to give yourself some quiet time away from your business. I know it's not easy to achieve, so book a morning or afternoon slot in your diary — it's the only way that this will actually happen. I speak from experience!

Think through where you are *right now* and assess your current level of satisfaction.

You can then determine what you need to do to move forward.

SETTING YOUR GOALS

> *"Goal setting is a very important first step,*
> *but achievement is a continuous, lifelong process."*
> *- Jim Rohn*

As Jim Rohn suggests, ask yourself the questions below.

Think big! Don't let negative thinking stop you from dreaming!

Allow your mind to flow and come up with ideas for each question. Jot these ideas down — don't start organising them yet! One of my clients was stuck not knowing whether to continue concentrating on her main service within the business or whether to diversify. She carried out this exercise and it helped to give her clarity.

What would you *love* to do? What would you love to accomplish? What would you try if you were guaranteed to succeed?

1. What do I want to do? What is it that I have always been passionate about?

2. Who do I want to be? What have I always aspired to being?

3. What do I want to see? When I have reached my goal what will I see around me?

4. What do I want to have? When I reach my goal what will I have?

5. Where do I want to go? What is the next step I want to take?

I'm a firm believer in going with your gut instinct and your intuition. If you have a clear vision of how you want to feel in your business, then you will find it easier to achieve. Maybe you would want to feel proud, alive, content, or in control.

So I would add: 'How do you want to <u>feel</u>?'

Remember the credo of Walt Disney:

"Think. Believe. Dream. Dare."

HOW TO SET SUCCESSFUL GOALS

1. **Belief** — The first step to goal setting is to have absolute belief and faith in the process. Make your thoughts turn into reality. Know that if you work hard and others help you, you can achieve your goal. Obviously, there are days that you won't believe it can happen but keep going — maybe carry out a small task which will take you to your end goal.

2. **Visualise** — What do you want? Think of what you deeply desire in your life or where you want your company to be a year from now. What changes have to take place? The clearer you are, the easier it will be to focus on making it happen. Maybe make a vision board with your goals and pictures on there so you have a physical focus.

3. **Get it down!** — Writing down your goals is the key to success. Have them written down where you can see them every day, e.g. put them on the walls, desk, mirror, etc. This will help you focus on them. Use "I will" <u>not</u> "I would" as it's more effective. For example, *I will increase my income by 10% in one month.*

4. **Purpose** — Knowing why you want to achieve your goals is powerful. Identifying the purpose of your goal helps you recognise instantly why you want that particular goal and whether it's worth working toward. It will motivate you to achieve.

5. **Commit** — This is a step that can be overlooked but it is crucial. Write a few sentences about why and how you are committing to each goal; why it's important to you. This is crucial to achieving your goal and, without it, success is unlikely.

6. **Stay focused** — By focusing on your goals, you manifest. You may not know how you'll reach your goals but when you make a daily practice of focus, they become easier to reach.

SETTING YOUR GOALS

7. **Plan of action** — In order to achieve your goal you need a list of action steps. You may not know all the steps ahead of time but you will know the next steps that take you in the right direction. By writing out your actions and crossing them off when completed, this will motivate you to continue. This is even more important if your goal is big or challenging. You need to sit down on a regular basis and plan out how you're going to achieve your dream. Think through all of the details. Break the whole plan down into small, workable parts. Then set a timeframe for accomplishing each task.

> *"Our goals can only be reached through a vehicle of a plan in which we must fervently believe, and upon which we must vigorously act. There is no other route to success."*
> *- Pablo Picasso*

8. **No time like the present** — Think of something you can do right now that will get you moving toward fulfilling your goals. Even if it's just making a phone call, do it now. You will be surprised how taking this simple step gets you motivated and moving toward what you desire.

9. **Accountability** — Tell people about your goal as it will spur you on to achieve it. People will ask you how you are getting on. It makes the goal more powerful! It makes sense to have someone beside yourself who can provide valuable feedback and keep you motivated, like a friend or a mentor. For me, having Siân-Elin Flint-Freel on board as my proof-reader and editor when writing my books makes a big difference to my motivation.

10. **Review and celebrate** — Make it part of your day to review your goals and take action. This will help you to keep on track. Give yourself some rewards along the way. Give yourself a huge reward when you get there.

DON'T FORGET TO BE SMART

Your goals should be:

Specific — Your goal must be clear and well defined. This will provide you with focus and direction. For example, a goal which states "I will have a few more clients by the end of the month" isn't as specific as "I will have 10 more clients by the end of the month and thereby increase my turnover by 20%."

Measurable — Include precise amounts, dates and so on in your goals so you can measure your degree of success. If your goal is simply defined as "To increase income", how will you know when you have been successful? In one month's time, if you have a 10% increase or in two years' time, when you have a 20% increase?

Attainable — When setting a goal, it is important to keep a balance between setting a goal which is too easy or too hard. Know yourself and know whether a massive goal will stretch you to achieve more or demoralise you! The goal needs to be realistic yet challenging.

Relevant — Goals should be relevant to the direction you want your life and career to take. This will help you to stay focused. If you set goals from your life plan and are clear on where you are going then achieving your goals will be easier.

Have a deadline (Timely) — Your goals must have a deadline. When I started writing my first book, 'Accountants Don't Bite', I immediately posted my publication date on my Facebook page to keep my motivation high.

Goal setting requires time and preparation to make it successful. It is important to give yourself that time, as without goals you won't have the focus you need for your business.

Are your goals SMART?

	Action (tick)
Specific	
Measurable	
Attainable	
Relevant	
Timely	

SETTING YOUR GOALS

When you're satisfied with your list of long-term goals, read through the list once again. Then beside each item, write the number of years (one, three, five or ten years) that you believe it will take you to achieve that particular goal.

LONG-TERM GOALS		
Goals	Priority (1-5) 1 being the most important	Length of time (years)

BREAKING IT DOWN

	Answer
Start with your most important long-term goal and break it down into smaller actions.	
Will your business need to change to complete these actions and achieve the long-term goal? If so, how? Write down a detailed description of what the new business will look like. Focus on what type of business. When you open it, will you need premises? If so, how much space will you need? Will you need employees?	
Re-write this long-term goal with absolute clarity.	

SETTING YOUR GOALS

Why do you want to achieve this goal? Write down as much detail as possible.	
If you can't find a clear and convincing reason for this goal then ask yourself — is this goal important to me?	
Who will help me to achieve this goal and keep me motivated?	

Now you've done it for your most important long-term goal, go through your other goals, asking yourself the same questions.

> *"The new year stands before us, like a chapter in a book, waiting to be written. We can help write that story by setting goals."*
> *- Melody Beattie*

Good luck with setting and achieving your goals. I'd love to know how you get on! I personally find it useful to tell people what I'm trying to achieve.

TIME FOR YOU TO SET SUCCESSFUL SHORT-TERM GOALS

We have already established that goal setting will help you to focus on your business. So far we have concentrated on long-term goals.

Now it's time to set your own short-term goals. This could be that you want to publish a monthly newsletter for your business or contact at least 10 prospective clients in the next 2 months.

Make a start by writing down 3 goals you want to achieve in the next 3 months. Alongside each goal write a plan of action designed to help you achieve each goal. Make sure you decide when you are going to start and complete each action and, most importantly, how are you going to celebrate completing each one! Maybe you could go to the cinema, visit a friend or have a meal in a local restaurant.

\multicolumn{4}{c	}{SHORT-TERM GOALS (Next 3 months)}
Goal	Action(s)	By when	Celebration
1.			
2.			
3.			

CHAPTER 3

ORGANISING YOUR TIME

"How did it get so late so soon?"
– Dr Seuss

You're clear now on the goals you want to achieve but as I know well, you're more likely to be successful if you manage your time. You state on your goals when you want to start and complete each one; having good time management will help you to achieve this.

I recently sent out a business questionnaire and was surprised that every respondent listed time management as one of their biggest weaknesses and also named it as one of the main factors that was holding them back.

One respondent captured it in a nutshell:

Q: **What is your biggest business challenge?**
A: **Never having time to focus on longer term goals/business development.**

I think this is an issue for all of us — we spend so long working 'in' the business that we run out of time to work 'on' the business. We are more likely to prioritise any work that generates fees.

Instead, fix your *focus* so that you gain *clarity*. This will help you to concentrate on where you want your business to go. Focusing on something makes it more likely to happen.

> *"One reason so few of us achieve what we truly want is that we never direct our focus; we never concentrate our power."*
> *– Tony Robbins*

From your work in the previous chapter, you now know what you want to achieve and the goals you have set yourself. You may be saying, "But how am I going to find the time to achieve all this as well as keep my business going?" It may all seem a bit overwhelming but the key to success is good time management — which is so much easier when you have specific goals. A big goal or a vision can be split into smaller goals, which become more achievable. It may be easier (and more motivating) to find the time to achieve the smaller goals, which then contribute to realising your vision.

SET SMART GOALS:

The last chapter gave you detailed notes and examples of what these are — here is a reminder:

Specific   be as clear as possible

Measurable   ensure you will know when you've achieved it

Accountable   tell people your goals

Relevant   make it relevant to you and your business

Timely   set a deadline

You have already come up with a list of *what* you want to achieve in the next 12 months. You have been as specific as possible and, where relevant, have broken them down into actions. Now it is time to work out *when* you can set aside the time to achieve these goals.

PLAN YOUR TIME

Maybe use a matrix such as the one below:

	MUST DO THESE THINGS NOW	**MUST PLAN TIME TO DO THESE THINGS/ PUT TIME IN DIARY**
IMPORTANT		
NOT IMPORTANT	**DELEGATE IF POSSIBLE**	**ELIMINATE OR IGNORE**
	URGENT	*NOT URGENT*

A good idea is to plan time in your diary when you are going to work on your business. Stick to it and tell everyone that you can't be disturbed.

See below for an example of the kind of tasks I would enter in each quadrant:

	Submit accounts with a deadline today	Submit VAT return by month end
IMPORTANT		
NOT IMPORTANT	Filing/recording	Cold calls/emails
	URGENT	*NOT URGENT*

MANAGING YOUR TIME

At a recent Institute of Certified Practising Accountants (ICPA) course, Simon Chaplin suggested using a daily planner to help manage your time. To aid clarity, he mentioned taking some time the night before to write down the 3 things you want to concentrate on the next day. Then do these first — before opening your emails!

This means you are working to your agenda, not someone else's!

Emails are a definite time-waster and, as Martin Perry in his talk, 'Taming your inbox' stated, "Email is an interruption." I believe that a change in attitude to our emails will have a significant impact on our time management.

How much time do you spend pinging back to your emails when you are in the middle of a piece of work because you have had a notification that a new message has arrived in your inbox? Your concentration is then broken and, at best, it takes a few minutes for you to get back into the flow of what you were doing. At worst, you spend hours on something which is someone else's emergency because of their poor time management!

Martin Perry's tips:

1. Don't open your emails until 10:30am.

2. Read the email once and do something with it; if you can action it in 2 minutes, then do it.

3. Remember the 5 Ds:
    - Delete it
    - Do it now
    - Do it later
    - Delegate it
    - Decide to keep for future reference

4. Switch email off for an hour during the day and see how much more productive you are.

How do you find a bit more time in your already busy day? A great starting point is to record how long you spend on day-to-day activities, such as using social media and watching TV. Be honest — you'll only be fooling yourself otherwise!

All the social media platforms — Twitter, Facebook, LinkedIn etc —break concentration. I know these are all good tools for a business to use but you can be much more effective by looking at them once or twice a day only. Maybe plan a few posts at a time and programme them to appear?

Review this list of daily activities and think about how you waste time and what you can plan to do to save time. What strategies will help you?

Could you:
- turn off your email notifications?
- turn off social media notifications?
- focus on one task at a time and complete it before moving on to the next?
- set an automatic reply on email to say that you won't be available until the afternoon?
- set an automatic reply on your phone to say that you won't be available until the afternoon?

It's no good following something that works for someone else as it may not work for you. Go back to the questions you asked yourself in the first chapter and consider how and when you work best. Use this to come up with your own bespoke action plan.

TIME MANAGEMENT AND FINANCIAL PLANNING

Maybe one of the ways you waste time is not using your finance system as productively as possible. As this is frequently the case, I talk more about putting systems in place in chapter 4.

There are many ways to save time; one of my clients decided to spend a weekend changing all her payments to suppliers into direct debits. This took time to set up initially but now it saves a significant amount of time and most importantly she feels more organised. Once we feel more organised and in control we are more likely to tackle other aspects of our business. A win/win situation!

Several of my clients/colleagues plan to hold meetings by Skype instead of face to face. Obviously, this saves travelling time.

Could you prepare your sales invoices or enter your purchase invoices onto the computer once a month, rather than at different intervals or when you remember, to save time?

More ideas on how to streamline your accounting and save time:
- Consider outsourcing your bookkeeping.
- Reduce your paper-based systems.
- Keep your personal and business bank accounts separate.

Learn how to use your time in the most efficient way.

> *"Think ahead. Don't let day-to-day operations drive out planning."*
> *- Donald Rumsfeld*

GETTING TO GRIPS WITH TIME MANAGEMENT

Now that you've read this chapter, think about how you can improve your time management and do something about it now.

Write down 3 actions you're going to take to improve your time management in the next week.

1. _____

2. _____

3. _____

Now you have your time-management actions, review them and see if they're working. If you start doing some of the actions as habit, add some more actions. Soon you will be super-efficient!

CHAPTER 4

KNOWING YOUR NUMBERS

"'Know your numbers' is a fundamental precept of business."
- Bill Gates

Over my fourteen years of trading I've seen a lot of resistance to numbers. Business owners don't want to spend the time getting to grips with them. There is a feeling that if they keep ignoring them, then they will go away. Well, I'm afraid they won't! It's important to face up to them, but do it in your own way. There are things you need to do but do it the way you want to. But why are they important in the first place?

WHY DO YOU NEED TO KNOW YOUR NUMBERS?

1. As a decision-making tool
When you set up in business there will have been a plan and you will have had targets that you want to reach. If you put off your filing and recording then

you won't know how your business is performing and can't plan. For example, knowing whether you need to:
- change your prices (see pricing chapter for further information);
- review costs and see if any can be cut;
- outsource work instead of keeping it in-house; or
- approach a different market.

2. To forecast

If your numbers aren't up to date then you can't use them to forecast future income, expenditure, profits and corporation tax payable. Forecasting helps you to be prepared for the future and plan ahead with regard to any peaks or troughs.

Do you need to:
- take out a short-term loan to cover a shortfall?
- take out a loan to buy equipment?
- increase your marketing to improve your sales figures?

Note — if a loan is needed then the bank will need an up-to-date forecast.

3. For compliance

Whether you want to keep your numbers up to date or not, ultimately you will have to do it anyway! So take control of them now and give yourself peace of mind.

As a sole trader you have to prepare a self-assessment return and submit it annually by 31 January. However, if you prepare this earlier then you will know how much tax you need to pay or whether you will have a tax refund.

At the date of writing this book, Making Tax Digital (MTD) hasn't yet started but it will start from April 2019 for sole traders above the VAT registration limit (which is £85k in the tax year 2018/19). It is unlikely to be in place for other businesses before 2020 but it's worth planning ahead.

As a director of a limited company you are responsible for filing your accounts 9 months after your year end and paying your corporation tax 9 months and 1 day after your year end. As I say above, at the date of writing this book, MTD isn't planned to be in place for limited companies until at least 2020.

How would understanding your numbers help you and your business? Thinking about the difference it can make will motivate you to get started! Have a go at prioritising your reasons for becoming more savvy about your business figures.

GETTING TO GRIPS WITH MY NUMBERS

If I understood numbers better (prioritise the following by entering the relevant number in the box, 1 being the most important, or enter N/A):

- My business would be more effective ☐
- It would take my stress away ☐
- It would help me to grow my business ☐
- It would help me price effectively ☐
- It would make my business more tax efficient ☐
- It would help me to take control and make better decisions ☐

When running a business, it is quite tempting to cut down on costs by managing the finances yourself. Most new business owners do this and sooner or later they realize that it's a false economy. Financial aspects of a business can be complicated and they require a dedicated person to handle them. It needs just one person whose sole job is to manage, record and give advice to the business owner about finances. An accountant can be a guardian angel — an adviser and strategic consultant all rolled into one.

You may be wondering why you need to know your numbers if you have an accountant. That's what they are there for, right? Wrong! You still have to understand the numbers around your business — it is *your* business after all.

PUTTING SYSTEMS IN PLACE FOR NUMBERS

"All the tools, techniques and technology in the world are nothing without the head, heart and hands to use them wisely."
- Rasheed Ogunlaru

There are many systems you can use to manage and improve your businesses; these include spreadsheets and cloud accounting software. The main thing, which I have emphasised throughout the book, is that you understand and like the system as this means that you are more likely to keep it up to date. It also helps if the system is easy for you to follow, and even better if it doesn't take up much of your precious time! However, what works for one person may not be suitable for another. Yet again, do it in your own way!

For example, last year one of my clients started taking a picture of all his receipts and entering them in his QuickBooks application on his smartphone. He is happy that he can have all his bank statements and figures available immediately in a couple of clicks. But this system wouldn't work for another client, who is happier using and keeping his spreadsheets up to date. Why? Because he doesn't like using his phone. He doesn't understand software and doesn't want it on his phone. He is happier doing it on a large screen computer at home.

Why do we need a system?

- To be organised.
- To hit deadlines.
- To have information available.
- To make informed decisions.
- To see how our business is doing.

Cloud accounting

If you run your own business, then you need a set of business accounts. Limited companies, partnerships and sole traders alike all need to keep their books in order. With the changes expected to the UK tax system over the next five years there is an expectation that most businesses will have to implement a computerised accounting package. Nevertheless, if you prefer to use Excel spreadsheets, then that's fine too.

Why choose cloud accounting?

The biggest advantage is the flexibility of access. You can access your accounts from any PC and any location with internet access. You don't need a capital investment in servers or software, most providers charge a monthly subscription, typically around £20/month plus VAT.

You can give your accountant or bookkeeper access so they aren't waiting for you to download data. They can work on your accounts from their offices, saving them time and hopefully saving you money. There will also be a saving because there won't be time delays and postage costs due to having to post information.

Another advantage is that the software is always the latest version — you don't have to install updates. However, the downside is that if you have no internet access you cannot access your accounts. You are also reliant on the provider keeping your data safe and backed-up and you have to remember more passwords!

Which is the best package to choose?

The best package is the one that best suits your business. It is worth making the most of the free trials that most providers offer. Always choose the package you feel most comfortable with rather than the one an accountant or bookkeeper insists upon, especially if you are going to be using it.

Think about what you are going to use the software for and then this will help you to decide whether you need a basic receipts and payments package or a fuller one.

Consider whether you need an option to:
- prepare sales invoices,
- reconcile the bank and therefore you will need bank feeds, or
- have an up to date picture of debtors and creditors.

What about if you have a problem and need some help, would you prefer:
- telephone support, or
- email support?

Many packages have tiered pricing, depending on the functionality you need. Most packages also have mobile applications to make it even easier to access your accounts on the move. The mobile apps may not always have the full functionality of the web-based packages.

It is worth considering who holds the licence (and pays) for your software. Your accountant may be a member of a provider's partnership scheme and be able to offer you slightly lower monthly subscription fees. In this case, the accountant will be the licence holder.

A lot of the cloud packages have add-ons available, such as ReceiptBank, bank feeds, real time stock control and financial forecasting. Receiptbank allows you to scan receipts and posts them into the bookkeeping package. Many of the bookkeeping packages have some form of scanning for receipts, so it is worth seeing if this is suitable for your use before signing up to more expense.

Here is a summary of a selection of packages:

Xero

Xero was developed in New Zealand and launched in the UK in 2011. It is one of the biggest providers of online accounting. Xero is quite different to the traditional accounting packages, such as Sage. It is very intuitive and easy to pick up. One feature that seemed revolutionary at the time is the bank reconciliation. You can link Xero to your internet banking and perform much of your bank reconciliation with a few clicks of the mouse.

Monthly subscriptions start at £10/month + VAT for very small businesses (you can have 5 sales and 5 purchase transactions and 20 bank transactions per month) to £27.50/month for full functionality plus multiple currencies. The standard package is currently £22/month + VAT.

Xero can include a payroll module for £5/month for up to five employees — useful if you are comfortable running your own small payroll. It is worth bearing in mind that the HMRC PAYE Toolkit is free and will manage up to 10 employees.

QuickBooks

QuickBooks was developed in the US in 1983, and the cloud-based package was launched in 2011. The functionality is similar to Xero and the differences between the two packages pretty much boil down to personal preference or recommendation. QuickBooks is slightly cheaper than Xero, with the standard package currently £15/month +VAT. The payroll module is £1/month per employee.

QuickBooks has another package aimed specifically at the self-employed, which helps to produce accounts and the Self-Assessment return. This product is currently £6/month + VAT.

Sage Online

Sage is probably the most well-known accounting package in the UK. It has been the package of choice for accountants for over 30 years. The cloud package is a fairly new product for Sage. The standard package is currently £20/month and has the same functionality as Xero and QuickBooks, although there is no payroll module available. Sage does, however, produce dedicated payroll software and there is a cloud-based version available.

Kashflow

Kashflow is a slightly cheaper option, although compared to other packages it can seem a little ungainly. The starter package (for sole traders and very small businesses) starts at £7/month, and the standard package is currently £13/month. The payroll module is only available with the Business+ package at £18/month.

FreeAgent

FreeAgent is a new provider, only having launched in 2007, and is one of the more expensive cloud packages, but it does have a little more functionality. Each product is tailored to the specific accounting requirements for the type of entity.

The approach is to demystify accounting, whilst still being technically accurate. The products are classified as Sole Trader (£19/month), Partnership/LLP(£24/month) and Limited Company (£29/month).

Exact

Exact is a fairly new package to the UK, having traditionally concentrated on the Benelux (Belgium, the Netherlands and Luxembourg) market. The software is an integrated CRM and accounting solution, useful if you have a lot of interaction with your customers. Like many of the other software packages, there is the ability to link bank feeds and to scan receipts. The standard package is currently £19/month + VAT, but does not include being able to link to your internet banking. The advanced option includes foreign currencies, bank feeds and asset management and is currently £29/month + VAT.

BeanBalance

BeanBalance is a free cloud-based accounting package. The company charges accountants a fee to list their services on the website, which funds the software development. The software does not contain some of the more complex accounting features, such as bank reconciliation, but a small business with very basic accounting needs may find it a good solution.

Features include sales invoicing, expense claims and standard and flat rate VAT schemes. BeanBalance does not support EU VAT, nor has the ability to link bank feeds or have any add-ons.

This is just a selection of the solutions available and, as already mentioned, the best thing to do is try a few out to see which is most comfortable for you.

MAKING TAX DIGITAL (MTD)

Making Tax Digital introduced the requirement for certain VAT registered businesses to keep digital records and file their VAT returns by using software accepted by HMRC.

Rather than maybe considering this as another thorn in your side, is this an opportunity for you to look at your business system and start to use cloud accounting?

You must follow the MTD rules (of using digital records and functional compatible software) if your business' VAT taxable turnover is more than the VAT registration threshold (currently £85,000) for VAT periods starting on or after 1 April 2019. If your VAT taxable turnover subsequently falls below this amount you must continue to follow the rules.

The registration threshold for VAT is based on a cumulative figure over the year. Therefore you should check your turnover at the end of each month and if it is about to go over the threshold you should apply the MTD rules from the start of your next accounting period.

Functional compatible software is a software programme or set of compatible software progammes that must be able to:
- record and preserve electronic records in an electronic form,
- provide to HMRC information and returns from the electronic records in an electronic form and by using the Application Performance Interface platform, and
- receive information from HMRC.

Under MTD for VAT, functional compatible software must be used to maintain the digital records they ask for, calculate your return and submit it to HMRC via an Application Programme Interface (API).

An API is a set of standard commands that programmers can use to interact with an external system. These commands are used for performing common operations and mean that the developers don't have to write the code from scratch each time. I know, it's a lot to take in! To put it simply, it helps one application talk to another, so your software must be able to 'talk' to the HMRC.

The complete set of digital records to meet Making Tax Digital for business (MTDfB) requirements do not all have to be in one piece of software. If there is a digital link between the pieces of software, records can be kept in a range of compatible digital formats.

HMRC has taken account of accountants and software producer's feedback about MTD and is aiming to make the move to MTD as user friendly as possible.

It is important to find the system that works for you and your business. Completing the table on the next page will help to give you focus. Good luck!

> *"There is strength in numbers, but organizing those numbers is one of the great challenges."*
> *- John C Mather*

MY IDEAL SYSTEM

SHORT-TERM GOALS (Next 3 months)	
Goal	Action(s)
1. My ideal system would be: • Spreadsheets • Accounting software	✓ ☐ ☐
2. I will start researching the system I want to use for my business on:	
3. I will keep my figures up to date:	Each day/week/month *(Delete as appropriate)*
4. The most important figures I need highlighted are:	
5. Do I need to buy any different equipment/software to have my ideal system?	
6. What is my monthly budget for this equipment/software?	
7. I will use the information gathered to help me focus on _____ *goal*	

Now you know you can't ignore your numbers, but where do you start working on them?

WHERE TO START

- Find everything: including bank statements, sales invoices, purchase invoices and receipts, and bring your information up to date for the year you are working on.
- File everything in date order.
- Decide on your system — spreadsheet or accounting software.
- Record <u>all</u> transactions on your system.
- Use your figures from the system to prepare a budget (see budgeting chapter for help).
- Review your budget and use it to update your business plan for moving your business forward.

(See action plan at the end of this chapter.)

BUSINESS NUMBERS YOU NEED TO KNOW

It is imperative as a business owner that you not only ensure that your business is running smoothly but also that you know your *key* numbers. Knowing these numbers will mean you can keep your business on track and can forecast the ongoing financial success of your business. Ideally look at your numbers weekly, but monthly as a minimum.

Key numbers you need to know:

(Maybe not all of these are relevant and maybe you are on top of some already but not others.)

1. Cashflow
Remember that profit is important but cashflow is king!

Calculate your cashflow by deducting the operational expenses from the total sales of products/services.

$$\text{Cashflow} = \text{Total Sales} - \text{Operational Expenses}$$

Chapter 7 shows an example of a budget and the types of expenditure which would be incurred.

If the cash outflow is greater than the cash inflow it is important to review your expenses and reduce costs wherever possible. Maybe review your suppliers and see if you could receive the same service at a lower price — if you spend a lot on carriage, is using Hermes cheaper than Royal Mail?

Cashflow can be increased by collecting customer payments faster and agreeing longer terms to pay suppliers.

2. Gross margin
This is the figure you arrive at once you have deducted the cost of sales from your total sales

$$\text{Gross Margin} = \left(\frac{\text{Total Revenue} - \text{Cost of Sales}}{\text{Total Revenue}} \right) \times 100$$

The cost of sales figure is the total cost of delivering your product/service. For example: distribution costs, labour, carriage and direct material costs.

The factors influencing gross margins are evident when looking at specific industry averages. The gross margin will be different for every business and depend on the type of industry you are in.

For example, the legal service industry has, on average, a gross margin of 93 percent as it has low production costs. The car dealer industry, on the other hand, has large fixed costs associated with building up stocks. As a result, the average gross margin for the industry is only 14 percent.

If your gross margin is small, this will mean that you won't be able to cover your administration expenses. You will need to look at your costs and see if any cost savings can be made or consider increasing your prices (see Pricing chapter).

3. Net income
This figure is calculated by deducting all your expenses, including taxation, from your sales figure.

$$\text{Net Income} = \text{Total Revenue} - \text{All Expenses}$$

However, it is not adjusted for items such as depreciation.

This figure gives you a good idea of whether your business is making or losing money. I would review it monthly and also take account of seasonality.

$$\text{Net Profit Margin} = \left(\frac{\text{Total Revenue} - \text{Total Expenses}}{\text{Total Revenue}}\right) \times 100$$

Using the above calculation you can work out the net profit margin too.

Income statement for Company XYZ Ltd		
for the year ended December 31, 20XX		
Total Revenue		£100,000
Cost of Goods Sold		(£20,000)
Gross Profit		£80,000
Operating Expenses		
Salaries	£10,000	
Rent	£10,000	
Utilities	£5,000	
Depreciation	£5,000	
Total Operating Expenses		(£30,000)
Interest Expenses		(£10,000)
Taxes		(£10,000)
Net Profit		£30,000

Using the formula and the information above, we can calculate that Company XYZ's net profit margin as £100,000 - £70,000 = 30,000 and £30,000/£100,000 = 30%

4. The sales close ratio

For a business to be successful it needs to sell enough products/services. Therefore it is important to monitor your sales closely.

This ratio is calculated by dividing the numbers of sales proposals by the number of sales you actually close.

$$\text{Sales Close} = \text{Sales Proposals}/\text{Sales Closed}$$

How many do you actually win? You don't want this number to be too high or too low. If it's too high then you're not talking to enough prospects. This ratio can be improved by asking more specific detailed questions of your potential customers.

This ratio will be different for all businesses but it's worth keeping an eye on. Maybe if it's too high you could increase the number of prospects by going to networking meetings. Maybe if it's too low, think about why — could it be to do with pricing, not explaining your services well enough, not understanding customer needs?

5. Accounts receivable age analysis

As you know, making sales is essential but you need to get paid for making those sales. It is important to age the debtors in order to see how quickly you are getting paid. The average number of days it takes for customers to pay is calculated by dividing debtors by sales then multiplying by 365.

$$\text{Accounts Receivable} = (\text{Debtors}/\text{Sales}) \times 365$$

The smaller this number the better, as this means you are getting paid quickly. Therefore, you can reinvest the money or take it out of the business. I would not recommend giving people longer than 30 days to pay and if they will accept 14 days I would use this. The best way to improve it is to regularly review, weekly if possible, who owes you money and chase them so that you not only improve this ratio you also improve your cash flow!

6. The quick ratio

This shows the financial stability of a business and is often calculated by banks if you request a loan. It is calculated by a business's total current assets (bank accounts, debtors) divided by its current liabilities.

Quick Ratio = Current Assets/Current Liabilities

Obviously, the higher your assets the better, and your business will look healthier. If you have a big overdraft and long term loans with very few fixed or current assets your business will not look at all healthy and the bank will not want to increase your overdraft or loans.

A healthy quick ratio is greater than 1 and shows that a company has more cash available than the current money it owes.

Now you know the key types of numbers which are of use to your business, ask yourself:

To get the most out of my business, what do I need to know about my numbers?

1. _____
2. _____
3. _____
4. _____

And what actions do I now need to take?

1. _____
2. _____
3. _____

Good luck with your number crunching and remember to regularly file and record everything (at least monthly) and then it will become a habit. Remember you will need to be specific about which numbers you need to review and by when.

Also, set a deadline. At a recent presentation, one of the ladies said that all of her filing was in the spare bedroom and she ignored it by shutting the door. Her action after my presentation was to open the door. However, I did remind her, "Give yourself a deadline for doing this otherwise you won't do it".

It's very easy to get so involved in your day-to-day business that you ignore the numbers...but now do so at your peril! If you are still unsure of which numbers would be of most use to you in understanding your business, have a chat with an accountant to talk it through.

> *"What we fear doing most is usually what we most need to do."*
> *- Tim Ferriss*

MY ACTION PLAN FOR GETTING TO GRIPS WITH MY NUMBERS

Action	Completed ✓
1. Find everything and file in date order	
2. Decide on the most appropriate system for your business	
3. Record all transactions on your system on (date):	
4. I will review by budget on (date):	
5. Do I need to buy any different equipment/software to have my ideal system?	
6. Select the ratios most appropriate for your business from: • Gross margin • Net income • Sales close • Accounts receivable • Quick ratio	✓ ☐ ☐ ☐ ☐ ☐
7. Calculate the relevant ratios:	
• Gross margin	$\left(\frac{\text{Total Revenue} - \text{Cost of Sales}}{\text{Total Revenue}}\right) \times 100$
• Net income	Total sales – All expenses
• Sales close	Sales Proposals/Sales closed
• Accounts receivable	(Debtors/Sales) x 365
• Quick ratio	Current assets /Current liabilities
8. I will review my numbers monthly; starting on (date):	

CHAPTER 5

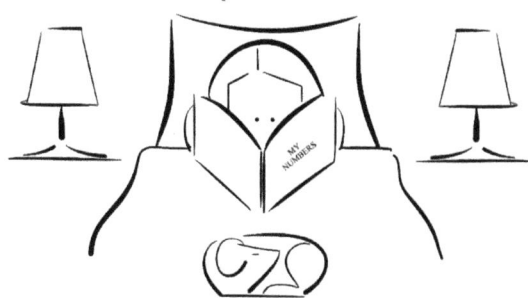

UNDERSTANDING YOUR ACCOUNTS

"Don't ever let your business get ahead of the financial side of your business. Accounting, accounting, accounting. Know your numbers."
- Tilman J. Fertitta

Now you know your numbers and how they impact on your business, the next stage is understanding how they impact on your accounts.

It is crucial for you to be able to read and understand your accounts. You know that you need to have accounts prepared each year to comply with Companies House rules. Maybe you feel that it is enough just to tick that box. But by not taking the time to understand you accounts you are missing a trick. In order to be able to grow a business and become more profitable it is essential to know the basics.

Obviously it is also important for you to understand your accounts if you are unincorporated, but for ease, in this chapter I have decided to use examples from limited company accounts.

All limited companies must file accounts with Companies House. These accounts are then available to the public. The most important financial statements are: the profit & loss account (P&L), the balance sheet and the cash flow statement. I don't cover the cashflow statement in this book as companies with a turnover of less than £10.2 million don't need to produce one.

In this chapter I will explain what a profit and loss account is and the main sections it includes. There are specific areas that a profit and loss account will not do, which I also touch on. This chapter examines the balance sheet and some specific ratios, as well as explaining what a director's loan account (DLA) is and investigating how cash differs from profit.

PROFIT AND LOSS ACCOUNT (P&L)

"The profit and loss statement tells you a lot about how your business is doing. It can also help you to determine ways that you can go about saving money so that you get to bring more money home! Basically, the P&L statement measures all of your income sources verses all your business expenses for any given period of time."
- Darren L Johnson

In its most simple form, the P&L tells you how much you've sold, how much you have bought and how much profit (or loss) you have made over a specific period of time – often a year, month, or quarter. As you can see from the balance sheet on page 55, it is the figure which is included under capital and reserves.

The P&L shows your business's income, less its day-to-day running costs.

The day-to-day running costs divide up into cost of sales (costs that relate immediately to sales) and administrative expenses (general running costs).

For example, the cost of buying materials to make goods to sell and the cost of delivering finished goods to customers would be cost of sales. Rent of an office would be an administrative expense. If your business sells services, it may not have any cost of sales.

Your business's income from sales is called turnover. Turnover less direct costs gives the **gross profit**, which we touched on in the previous chapter. A business's total income, less its day-to-day running costs, is its **net profit**. I'll say a bit more about this later in the chapter.

UNDERSTANDING YOUR ACCOUNTS

The profit & loss account will state what the total operating profit figure is. The charge for corporation tax is typically this figure multiplied by the tax rate after adding back items such as depreciation and entertaining, which are not tax deductible.

Corporation tax is paid on the company's income and capital gains, usually nine months after the company's year end.

The notes to the profit and loss account give the user more information regarding what has been included under a heading, for example the 'taxation on profit' note could include both corporation and deferred tax. The 'turnover' note explains the basis used to calculate turnover and the 'operating profit' note shows what is included to arrive at the operating profit figure. The numbers provided under the heading reference a specific note.

The profit for the financial year is the one which is included on the balance sheet under capital and reserves.

Here is an example of a typical P&L account for a small limited company:

Profit and loss account for the year ended 30 April 2018

	Notes	2018 £	2017 £
Turnover	2	384,821	240,350
Cost of sales		89,965	44,942
Gross profit		294,856	195,408
Administrative expenses		19,829	36,628
Operating profit	3	275,027	158,780
Other interest receivable and similar income		-	103
Profit on ordinary activities before taxation		275,027	158,883
Taxation on profit on ordinary activities	5	57,059	33,267
Profit for the financial year		217,968	125,616

THE MAIN SECTIONS OF A PROFIT AND LOSS ACCOUNT

Most P&L accounts are put together in a similar way, although the detail of what's included in each section may vary from one business to another.

1. Turnover
   Turnover, or sales, is the total value of what you've sold during the period net of VAT. It might be broken down into different types of product, helping you to see which items sell better than others.

   Other income received by the business, such as bank interest or money received from the sale of assets, is not included in turnover because it does not represent income from your main trading activity.

2. Cost of Sales
   These are the costs that are directly related to the sales you have made, so it includes raw materials or stock you have purchased to resell. It may also include the cost of creating the items that you sold, including the cost of staff time if you are selling services.

3. Gross Profit
   This is the sum of Turnover minus Cost of Sales. It tells you how much profit you are making directly from your sales.

4. Administrative expenses
   These are all the other costs associated with running a business, such as the rent and rates on your premises, accountancy and legal fees, and depreciation. These costs cannot be directly linked to your sales and may not change very much even if your sales figures were to change significantly.

5. Profit for the financial year
   This is the Gross Profit minus the administrative expenses. You could think of it as the true profit of your business because it's made up of all the income and all the costs.

WHAT A PROFIT AND LOSS ACCOUNT WILL NOT DO

The P&L is a relatively easy document to understand, which is why it's the first one that many people look at when assessing the health of a business.

But it's important to understand its limitations. The P&L will not tell you about the underlying health of the business, such as how much money it owes or is owed and what the value of its assets are.

The P&L will show you whether a business is making a profit but not whether it's generating cash. If that appears to be a contradiction, it's not, because a business might sell lots of goods at a good margin, but if it fails to collect payment from its customers — that profit is worthless.

Companies that are profitable on paper can still suffer major cash flow problems. That's why every business, from start-ups to established firms, needs to plan carefully where the cash is going to come from to buy stock, to pay wages and to settle outstanding tax bills.

BALANCE SHEET

A **balance sheet** is a financial statement that summarizes a company's assets, liabilities and shareholders' equity at a specific point in time; usually on the last day of a company's financial year. These three balance sheet segments give investors an idea as to what the company owns and owes, as well as the amount invested by shareholders. It also gives the business owner a good overview of the state of their business.

The top half of the balance sheet starts with the business's assets (what the company owns). These are divided into **fixed assets** (e.g. computers and furniture), **tangible assets** (assets that have a physical form) and **current assets,** which are assets that are more easily and quickly converted into cash, e.g.
- Bank
- Petty cash
- Trade debtors (money owed by customers)
- Stock
- Prepayments (items paid in advance, for example, insurance paid for a year, but only half relates to this specific financial period — 50% would be prepaid)

The balance sheet then shows the business's liabilities (what the company owes), which divide into **current liabilities** and **long-term liabilities**. Current liabilities are money due within a year e.g.
- Tax bills
- Money owed to staff

- Trade creditors (money owed to suppliers)
- Accruals (items outstanding at the period end, e.g. accountant's bill not invoiced)
- Long-term liabilities are due in more than a year, like a mortgage or bank loan.

There will then be a total of all the business's assets less its liabilities. If the business were to sell all its assets off, and pay all its debts, anything left over would be available for the business's owner(s) to draw out. That's why the bottom half of the balance sheet is headed up **'Shareholders' Funds'** (made up of issued share capital and reserves). **Issued share capital** is the total of a company's shares that are held by shareholders. **Called up share capital,** included under the heading of capital and reserves on the next page, is the amount of a company's capital which has been paid for by people who have bought shares.

The total of the bottom half of the balance sheet will equal the top half. These two totals are called the balance sheet total.

The notes heading refers to notes provided by the accountant which are a breakdown of the specific items. The numbers provided under the heading reference a specific note.

The fixed assets note will show a breakdown of the total cost brought forward adjusted for any additions or disposals and the depreciation brought forward and charged in the year.

The debtors figure could include trade debtors and prepayments.

The called up share capital note shows the amount of share capital paid for by the people who have bought shares.

The profit and loss note shows the opening profit figure with this year's profit or loss added or subtracted from it.

Here is an example of a typical balance sheet for a small limited company:

Balance sheet at 30 April 2018			
	Notes	2018 £	2017 £
Fixed assets			
Tangible assets	6	**3,214**	1,284
Current assets			
Debtors	7	91,904	39,638
Cash at bank and in hand		160,468	38,262
		252,372	77,900
Creditors: amounts falling due within one year		(146,878)	(60,444)
Net current assets		105,494	17,456
Total assets less current liabilities		108,708	18,740
Capital and reserves			
Called up share capital	9	100	100
Profit and loss account	10	108,608	18,640
Shareholders funds		108,708	18,740

If your business owns more than it owes, then the balance sheet total will be a positive figure. If your business owes more than it owns, the balance sheet total will be negative — and that's not good news, because it means your business doesn't have enough money available to pay its debts.

As you can see, the balance sheet and P&L aren't just for your accountant! You can use them to collate a lot of useful information about your business's financial health, and to help you make essential business decisions.

RATIOS

The figures included on the balance sheet and profit & loss account can be used to prepare ratios which give us more information about the business. I covered some ratios in chapter 4, but here are some more specific ones for investors. However, they still give the business owner useful information about their business, even if they are not looking for investment.

The debt-to-equity ratio
As we have seen, a company's assets can be sourced in two ways — from creditors in the form of loans and other liabilities, and from shareholders in the form of share capital and retained profits.

The ratio of these two is a key measure of a company's strength because debts can always be called in by a creditor, while the shareholders' equity is forever.

A company with high levels of debts compared with shareholders' funds is said to be highly 'geared' or highly 'leveraged'.

Many people have experienced this ratio in a personal capacity when they took out a mortgage to buy a house. A borrower will be able to access funds more cheaply if they have a big deposit relative to the amount of money they want to borrow.

In balance sheet terms, they have a lower debt-equity ratio and lenders consider them a lower risk as a result. The same is true of companies.

The debt to equity ratio is expressed like this:

$$\text{Debt to Equity} = \text{Total Liabilities}/\text{Total Shareholders' Funds}$$

There is no 'correct' level of gearing and the appropriate level will vary from industry to industry so it is best to compare the debt-equity ratio with comparable companies in the same sector. The industry averages can be found by subscribing to Industry Watch by Merlin Scott Associates Ltd.

Return on equity
Another key measure for investors is how hard a company is working the assets at its disposal. Wherever it has sourced its assets from borrowings or from shareholders' funds, it needs to generate an acceptable return on those assets.

At the very least it needs to earn more from the capital it has invested than its cost in the form of interest payments on debts and dividends on equity.

Many investors consider return on equity to be the key determinant of whether or not a company is worth investing in.

To calculate the return on equity you need to look at both the balance sheet (for the equity) and the income statement (for the return).

The return on equity is then calculated as follows:

Return on Equity = Net Total Income/Total Shareholders' Equity

Again there is no 'right' return on equity, so the best thing to do is to compare the return against:
- risk-free returns — why would you take the risk of investing in a business if it was returning no more than a deposit account, for example?
- the returns from other similar companies
- the returns from the same company in recent years — you should worry if returns are declining and ask why that might be the case

DIRECTOR'S LOAN ACCOUNT (DLA)

As a director of a limited company, one of the concepts which is difficult to get your head around is the DLA.

A director's loan is when you take money out of your company that isn't a salary, dividend or expense repayment and you've taken more than you've put in. The DLA shows all amounts you have entered into the business or items paid personally and all amounts you have withdrawn.

If the figure you withdraw is greater than the amount you have entered the DLA becomes overdrawn and you pay tax on it at 32.5%.

Example

	£
Cash introduced by director	5,000
Less withdrawals	6,000
Add expenses paid personally	500
Overdrawn balance	500
Tax at 32.5%	162.50

Once the loan is repaid in full you can request for this amount to be refunded. Tax won't be paid if the loan is repaid in full 9 months after your year end. As you can see, this is an important point as you can easily end up paying this 32.5% on top of your corporation tax charge. A big impact on cashflow!

CASH VERSUS PROFIT

Cash is like air; profit is like food. You need cash all the time, but you can survive — for a while — without profit.

Certainly, profit is essential for a business to grow. If there is no profit being generated over the long-term, the company will disappear. But also, it is a fatal mistake to overlook your cash position. Cash is necessary for the short-term survival of the firm.

CASH VS. PROFIT EXAMPLE

Suppose you're making sales of £100 and you pay for stock of £50 and have other expenses of £40. This leaves you with £10 as profit. You're pleased; you're running a profitable business, and you think if you double everything you'll make twice as much.

However, in order to make a sale, you'll also need larger stocks. Currently, you have stock worth £200 and you're making sales and using £50 of that stock in the sales. Now, for the larger sale, you have to put another £200 in to have twice as much stock, you may have to rent some additional space to store it, and you may need to spend more on finding clients… and the money for all that goes out before you've made any additional sales.

Your sales might go up to £200, but your cost of sales increases to £100. Your profits may be double or more, but the money you had to pay for extra stock and to recruit and train salespeople and any other costs has increased and gone out months before you start selling — not to mention the fact that some people don't pay until months after a sale. We have to make sure we have a strong enough cash flow to cover the period while not being paid.

HOW TO PAY ATTENTION TO BOTH CASH AND PROFIT

Avoiding a critical oversight of either cash or profit requires multiple things:

1. **You need a strategic plan**
   Where do you want to go? Where would you like to be? This is the 'dreamer' or vision phase of business planning; it's necessary, though certainly not enough to fuel a business.

2. You need a budget

You can use your P&L from the last six months to determine a budget for the next six months.

You must determine whether the business can be profitable before you even worry about cash flow. Without profit, a business will never survive long-term.

3. You need a cash flow forecast

Budgets tell you if your expansion will be profitable, and how much profit you will make. But they don't tell you when cash is coming in. That's where the cash flow forecast comes in.

Once you have a grasp on how to handle your cash flow needs, a) your own expectations will be as realistic as can be, and b) banks and investors will look more favourably on your business. They will know they're dealing with someone who understands business.

You should be looking at least a year down the road to know when and where money is going out and where it will come in from. That way, you'll know how much money will have gone out before your profitable sales start. It'll tell you how much fresh funding you'll need beyond the profits of the business and when you can afford to start your expansion if you're going to self-fund.

The bottom line:

Cash is not profit, and profit is not cash. You need both to sustain and grow a business, though not in equal measures at every point.

But you never start with the cash flow.

The vision starts a business, profitability helps it grow, and cash flow is the day-to-day driver.

As long as you have enough cash to survive, you can comfortably expand to a more profitable business.

> *"We cannot become what we want to be by remaining what we are."*
> *- Business guru Max DePree*

Good luck with starting to understand your accounts. Remember, if you haven't reviewed your accounts before, it will be a skill you need to perfect. Complete the table below to give you focus and don't be afraid to ask questions. That's what your accountant is there for!

MY ACTION PLAN FOR UNDERSTANDING MY ACCOUNTS

	Action
1. When is my current year end?	
2. When will my final accounts be ready for review?	
3. I will review my accounts on (date):	
4. Select the ratios most appropriate for your business from: • Gross margin • Net income • Sales close • Accounts receivable • Quick ratio • Debt to equity • Return on equity	✓ ☐ ☐ ☐ ☐ ☐ ☐ ☐
5. When looking at my accounts the figures which are particularly relevant to me are:	
6. The questions for my accountant after reviewing my accounts are:	

CHAPTER 6

PRICING YOUR WAY TO BUSINESS SUCCESS

""The moment you make a mistake in pricing, you're eating into your reputation or your profits."
- Katharine Paine

In the questionnaire I sent out recently asking about people's business challenges, as well as time management being an issue, one of the other biggest ones is pricing! I also know this from the mentoring sessions I give as this is an area business owners frequently need help with.

In order to have a successful business then it's crucial to get the pricing right in order to ensure you are covering all costs and achieving the profit margins you want. Some businesses don't realise their mistake with pricing and others do but don't correct it quickly enough. The Four Ps of the Marketing Mix demonstrates why pricing is so important for overall business success.

THE FOUR PS OF THE MARKETING MIX

1. Product
Your product is for many reasons the first and most important part of your marketing mix. Your product can be a good or a service, or a combination of the two, and it in some valuable way fulfils a customer's needs or wants.

In order to set your marketing strategy correctly, and specifically your pricing strategy, you need to be fully aware that you know the ins and outs of your product.

If you have that clear grasp of what your product is, how it helps people and what makes it unique, you can market it successfully.

2. Pricing
This is one of the biggest selling points for your product (besides the perceived value the product brings). Your price will impact your profit margins, supply and demand, and your marketing strategy.

While the value of your product is related to your skills and understanding of what is needed in the market, the pricing strategy you employ can be calculated to impact positively on these other factors.

The strategy will also affect how you handle the remaining two Ps.

3. Promotion
When you've set your product and your pricing strategy, you need to work to promote it.

The most important part of your promotion, of course, is to present your product's value and differentiate it from that of a competitor. You will need to know your customer and your ideal potential customers in depth. Who are they? Where do they buy from? What sort of language do you need to use to encourage them to buy?

Promotion will include advertising in magazines including trade magazines, marketing on social media, email, public relations and a lot more.

4. Place
Although the common saying is "the right place at the right time," marketers tend to state it differently: "the right product, at the right price, at the right place and the right time."

Place is also crucial to finding success with your product. If you've got the perfect product, price and promotion, but you put it in the wrong place, you will experience failure. For example, if you are selling expensive beauty products, you need these displayed in a department store not a supermarket.

It's necessary to determine exactly where your ideal clients are congregating, and how, in order to successfully market your product.

Nowadays, this ideal location is mostly online, but with the size of the web it is still a difficult task.

Business owners often realize they have pricing issues at one of two times. The first is when the bank balance is low. The second is during tax time and they have nothing set aside to pay the tax bill for the year. Wouldn't it be better to be forewarned and be able to do something about it now?

Things to think about:

What is the purpose of your pricing? What do you hope to accomplish?

Knowing your goals will help you better determine which pricing strategy to use.

There are usually four pricing goals:
- **To maximize profit**: to improve current profits, as opposed to long-term profits.
- **To maximize revenue**: to maximize current revenue without consideration for profit margins, and the intention is usually to maximize long-term profits.
- **To maximize quantity**: to sell as many units as possible or serve as many people as possible in order to decrease long-term costs.
- **To have price equilibrium**: to find a steady price in order to avoid potential price wars and to have stable profits. Equilibrium price is the price at which the exact quantity that producers take to market will be bought by customers.

For example, an experiment was undertaken to see how many soft drinks students would buy at a certain price. It was found that the price equilibrium was 60p per soft drink. At this price, the demand for drinks by students equals the supply: 500 drinks will be offered for sale at 60p and 500 will be bought.

Small business owners can ensure profitability and be able to continue in business by paying close attention to their pricing strategy. There are many pricing strategies that can be used, for example: lowest price, cost-plus and customer perceived value. These and others will be discussed later in the chapter.

PREPARATION

The most important aspect is the **preparation**; some questions you need to answer are:

Do you understand your product and distribution? Are you dealing with a basic or a premium product?

Do you understand your ideal customer well enough? Who do you want to attract? Do you understand the market well enough?

Do you understand your product or service well enough, including *all* associated costs?

Who are your competitors and have you checked your competitors' pricing? Can you distinguish yourself from the competition?

What is the image you want to display?

Preparation steps

1. **Understand your product and distribution**
   You need to know what your product is, who it is for and how it brings value.

   You should also understand how your product or service will be distributed to the customers as this will affect the cost and amount of time it takes the product to arrive with the customer.

2. **Determine customer demand**
   This is applicable both for businesses with existing products hoping to adjust the prices and businesses just starting out.

   You need to have a good idea of what the effect of your price will be on sales by estimating how the demand will fluctuate with the price.

Existing businesses can sometimes experiment with small but significant segments of customers and see the impact. It will be a case of deciding on a percentage you want to try this on — say 20% of your customers who buy regularly — and noting what they were prepared to pay and whether they bought if you increased the price by 10%.

Price affects sales. Lowering the price of a product increases customer demand. However, too low a price may lead customers to think you are selling a low quality 'budget product'.

3. Determine product and service costs

In order to determine if you'll make a profit from your product or service, you need to calculate the costs involved.

Your total costs should be the lower limit of what you should be charging and anything above that will be your profits.

There are two costs when it comes to your product or service:

The first is **fixed costs**, which will be a certain amount regardless of how much or little of your product you actually produce. Fixed costs include:
- office rent;
- insurance,
- equipment,
- interest on debt (loans), and
- employee salaries.

This list will vary depending on your business.

The second is **variable costs**, which will increase with each additional unit being produced. These include production labour time, materials and packaging.

In a recent mentoring session I helped a client to prepare her initial cash flow forecast in order to receive a bank loan. She was surprised that all of her costs had to be included when calculating her selling price rather than just variable costs. I explained that she also needed to cover her premises rent, insurance and any loan interest.

4. Understand competitor influences

While you may be able to determine your price based on your costs, that is unfortunately not the way the market works.

The competitor's price should also be taken into account when determining your own price. In addition, you should continue watching competitor pricing afterwards, as your competitors may lower their prices. This should be done regularly, at least weekly, sometimes even daily.

Be aware that setting a price above that charged by the market leader can only work if your product has better features and appearance. The level of customer service you provide will make a big difference too. Also, if you give added value then this can be something worth paying extra for compared with your competitors.

PRICING STRATEGIES

In order to achieve your pricing goals there are many pricing strategies you can use. Here are some:

Lowest price
The advantage to this method is it is clear to the customer. But there are also many disadvantages. Customers in most cases are driven by factors other than price. Price may get someone in the door the first time, but without a clear benefit, people probably will go back to business owners with whom they have a longstanding relationship. People switch for better products, services or customer service, not cost.

I have seen this done for networking events where the cost is very little but it is unsustainable for the organiser and frequently people don't bother to turn up as they don't value the event.

Cost-plus
This involves calculating the cost to make your product, then adding a flat amount or a percentage for overhead and profit (margin).

For example, adding a 50% mark up to a sandwich that costs £2 to make means setting the price at £3. This should avoid the problem of under-pricing so that you run out of cash. But it doesn't take the competition into account. It also does not take into account that you may have a premium product, offer an experience to your customer or provide another value-added element for which people will pay extra.

The drawback of cost-plus pricing is that it may not be competitive and, of course, lower priced goods will bring in less and therefore the quantity sold will need to be higher.

Industry mark-ups

Industry mark-ups (mark-ups in specific industries) should help ensure you make a profit, but they don't look at how competitive you might be. Mark-ups vary enormously from industry to industry. In some industries, the mark-up is only a small percentage of the total cost of the product or service. Companies in other industries, however, are able to attach a far higher mark-up.

For example, in the restaurant industry, food is generally marked up about 60%, and some beverages may be marked up as much as 500%. Nevertheless, because restaurant overhead costs are high, profits in the industry are extremely low compared to other industries, averaging less than 5% of sales and, in some specific sectors, such as retail fast food, going as low as 2.5%.

Customer Perceived Value (CPV)

It basically is a combination of the other methods, along with an understanding of where your product sits, in the customer's eyes.

> *"Price is what you pay. Value is what you get."*
> *- Warren Buffett*

This pricing strategy requires you to do your research. You need to figure out first of all what the perceived value of your product is to the customer compared to competing products.

Customer perceived value can be calculated as:

$$CPV = \text{Total Perceived Benefits} - \text{Total Perceived Costs}$$

The CPV here would be a monetary conversion of the benefits of any product or service.

For example, if a customer buys a car, besides the usual uses of a car, the benefits can include his/her feeling of excitement when driving it, the adoration or envy from his/her friends and family, and many others.

If he/she believes the benefits in total equal £25,000, and the total costs to produce the car come to £14,000, the seller will have to decide which price to offer based on the CPV.

The lower the price, the higher the benefits, the higher the CPV and the higher the incentive to purchase.

The higher the price, the lower the CPV, and the seller can price himself out of the market at too high a price. Therefore, at a price of £23,000, the CPV is £2,000 and could be enough incentive for the customer to make the purchase.

One of my clients needed to use a solicitor to buy a property and met up with two possible options. The lady solicitor was more expensive but she was more experienced and helpful so he chose her rather than the cheaper one. He felt that it was worth paying more for the added value.

You would, of course, also need to take into account the competition to help you determine the price.

Competitive pricing
This is the most common and should be utilized in some form regardless of what pricing strategy you ultimately go with.

First, you need to make a survey of your competitors' pricing, then calculate the average or mean. From that, you can decide to go below their base prices or stay at the same level. Make sure when carrying out the comparison you use the same units — hourly or per unit.

This, of course, has to take into account your own costs. For this to be effective, your cost structure should be similar to your competitors', or else you could be under-pricing your products.

Garden centres with similar sized premises and overheads frequently charge an almost identical price for their cream teas.

Competitive pricing is also common with franchises, such as McDonald's and Burger King, so they are able to be competitive and profitable.

Psychological pricing
This is based on the idea that pricing can be used to affect perceptions of quality, fair value, savings and more. Charm pricing and prestige pricing are examples of this.

> *"All our knowledge has its origin in our perceptions."*
> *– Leonardo da Vinci*

Charm pricing. This is a common pricing strategy for retailers and supermarkets. Here, the prices will normally end in '9' or '99'.

The left digit is simply reduced from a round number in order to induce customers to buy more based on the way our brain works, for example £1.00 to 99p.

Specifically, our brains see that £5.00 and £4.99 are different prices, although much more drastically than we think. To our brains, £4.99 is £4.00, which is much cheaper than £5.00.

Charm pricing is frequently used by petrol stations.

Premium/prestige pricing. This strategy is based on the idea that higher prices can convince the customer that the product or service has high value.

There are many psychological aspects involved in this persuasion, including the exclusivity the price offers. The availability of the product or service should also be limited, which improves its exclusivity.

It is important to state, however, that the brand should usually be strong for premium pricing to be effective. e.g. Apple products and designer clothes.

SEVEN BIGGEST MISTAKES IN SETTING PRICES

Setting prices is challenging, not only to a start-up, but also to well-established businesses, especially those in lower-margin, highly competitive industries, for example, supermarkets. The common theme with most pricing issues is risk: risk setting prices too high and you may push potential customers away; risk setting prices too low and you cut profits.

Keep reviewing your prices.

> *"The price of inaction is far greater than the cost of making a mistake."*
> *-Meister Eckhart*

In order to decrease these risks it's best to get as much information as you can about your market, your customers and your own numbers.

Here are 7 mistakes to avoid making:

1. Pricing too low and undercutting all the time. Going in too low all the time can have a great effect on your turnover figure, but it can destroy your net profit and this is the one you will need to survive! You need to profit and price accordingly. If you price your products too low, you may cause your products to appear too cheap. It can also harm the brand, as many people will then associate the brand as being low quality compared to your competitors.

For example, Ryanair. Low pricing may destroy your business if it is not enough to cover costs. This is especially true if your sales volume goes down.

2. Using the same margin for all products. In reality, slower moving, more expensive items need higher profit margins. You can afford a smaller margin on cheaper products based on high sales volume. Even then, you should find ways to add value and increase those margins.

3. Not understanding the difference between margin and mark-up. Margin is always based on sales price. Mark-up is always based on cost.

4. Forgetting to take all costs into account. In order to price correctly — *every* cost needs to be identified, e.g. credit card processing fees and delivery costs.

Have you included all your costs in your pricing?

Fixed costs	• Office rent • Insurance • Loan interest	• Salaries • Advertising • Broadband
Variable costs	• Salaries • Materials • Packaging	• Credit card/PayPal fees • Delivery costs

5. Finding out what your competition charges and doing the same. Price for value. Then you can defend your price against the competition, with a list of why your offering is worth its price.

6. Setting sales commissions based on sale prices vs. percentage of profit. Commission based on turnover vs. commission based on the net profit directly impacts profitability. It means that the commission that is being paid out does not cover any costs of the business. Again, profit is the only number that matters.

7. Discounting instead of adding value. Discounting takes a toll on profits. At just a 10% discount, a typical firm would need to sell 50% more units to keep the same profit on the bottom-line. Instead of discounting, ask yourself if there is a way you can add value to your product or service, maybe by the level of customer service offered or by offering better features. If you do decide to make a special offer then make sure it's for a limited time period to encourage customers to buy. If there is no deadline then there is no urgency for the customer and they forget to buy it!

Lowest pricing does not win, as I explained in point 1, but nor does pricing too high. If you price your products too high, your customer's perception of value for the product may end up suffering, or they may go to a competitor with a better price and value.

Of course, whether a high-priced item will survive or not depends on *how elastic the product is* — how sensitive customers are to a change in price.

If it is highly elastic, even a small increase in price will have huge effects on demand, such as coffee or airline tickets. A product with low elasticity means that price increases do not affect demand much, such as for cigarettes or fuel.

You need to be aware of how elastic the demand for your product or service is. Unfortunately for most business owners, products are likely to be highly elastic.

I have mentioned services as I have gone through this chapter, but remember that when you price for services you must take account of your experience. The time taken to prepare a piece of work isn't the relevant cost, it's the value the customer will receive from it and the years it's taken you to gain the relevant experience.

Trying to avoid making these pricing mistakes will make a big difference to the success of your business and you'll be more competitive.

There is a lot to take into account when deciding on your prices. The key to success is to know your pricing goals and prepare adequately. Remember, none of the pricing strategies will be as effective in isolation; use a combination of those which are most suitable for your business.

PRICING IS KEY TO BUSINESS SUCCESS

It is essential to decide on the prices you are going to charge in your business and review them regularly. In order to do this it's best to get a plan in place.

It's important to get the balance for you, your business and your customer. Research is important to get this correct!

MY ACTION PLAN FOR PRICING

	Action
1. My product/service is: and is used by: and brings value to customers by: It is a (delete as appropriate)	Basic/premium product/service
2. My product/services will be distributed to customers by: (method used)	
3. My ideal customer is (be as specific as possible):	
4. My 3 main competitors are:	
5. I will review my competitor's prices on (date):	
6. I am different to my competitors because:	
7. I will make a _____% change to my pricing on _____ to _____% of my customers and note the impact, if any.	
8. I will make a list of all my costs (both fixed and variable) on (date):	
9. My pricing goal is:	
10. My pricing actions are:	
11. I will review my prices monthly; starting on (date):	

CHAPTER 7

BUDGETING FOR YOUR SUCCESS

"A budget is telling your money where to go instead of wondering where it went."
- Dave Ramsey

WHAT IS A BUDGET?

A budget can be for business or personal use but this chapter will focus on budgeting for your business because I will talk about personal budgeting in chapter 9.

> A budget is a financial plan used to project future income and expenditure. It is a tool to achieve financial control in a business and helps to evaluate performance and formulate plans.

We hear the word 'budget' on an almost daily basis. Whether you are trying to monitor your business performance or planning for the launch of a new product or service, it is important for you to understand why you need a budget and how to go about preparing one to meet your business needs.

WHY DO WE NEED ONE?

There are a number of benefits to drawing up a business budget, including being better able to:
- manage your money effectively,
- monitor performance,
- meet your objectives,
- improve decision-making,
- identify problems before they occur — such as the need to raise finance or cash flow difficulties, and
- plan for the future.

EXCUSES FOR NOT PREPARING A BUDGET

Over the 14 years that I've been trading, I've heard lots!
- It's too depressing.
- What's the point?
- Don't have the time.
- Don't know where to start.
- I can enter the expenditure but I can't predict the income.

It's so easy to make excuses and not prepare a budget but having one has a massive positive impact on your business. It is part of your planning for business success.

> *"The budget is not just a collection of numbers, but an expression of our values and aspirations."*
> *- Jacob Lew*

PREPARING A BUDGET

Decide firstly on the period you want the budget to cover — this is normally for 12 months but it can be up to 3 years if you want to grow your business and therefore set future goals. I would recommend that you start from just after your year end and finish 12 months later. For example, my year end is 30 June so I would start on 1 July and finish on 30 June. All companies will have different year ends. A sole trader often has a year end which finishes on 31 March to coincide with the tax year.

It need not be complicated. You simply need to work out what you are likely to earn and spend in the budget period. Before we start, I know one of your comments is likely to be, "How on earth do I know what my income will be in the next twelve months?" Well, I will tackle that first!

Begin by gathering all the information you'll need to answer these questions:

- What are the **projected sales** for the budget period? Often this is a sticking point as it's unknown but give it a go and be realistic. Maybe conduct some market research to discover the quantity of your product/service you are likely to sell each week and then multiply over the year. Remember to take account of any seasonality.

- What are the **direct costs** of sales? i.e. costs of materials and subcontractors to make the products or supply the service.

- What are the **fixed costs** or overheads?

You should break down the **fixed costs** and **overheads** by type, e.g.:
- Cost of premises, including rent and council tax
- Staff costs e.g. wages and national insurance
- Utilities e.g. heating and lighting
- Printing, postage and stationery
- Motor expenses
- Insurance
- Equipment costs
- Advertising
- Telephone
- Travel and subsistence expenses
- Legal and professional costs
- Directors' remuneration
- Dividends
- Provision for tax

Please enter your costs in the table below.

PREPARING YOUR BUDGET — TOTAL COSTS

	Costs	Amount (£)
1	Premises costs	
2	Staff costs	
3	Utilities	
4	Printing, postage and stationery	
5	Motor expenses	
6	Insurance	
7	Equipment costs	
8	Advertising	
9	Telephone	
10	Travel and subsistence	
11	Legal and professional	
12	Director's remuneration	
13	Dividends	
14	Provision for tax	

This list can be added to depending on your particular business. For example, driving instructors might need to include franchise fees.

Once you've got figures for income and expenditure, you can work out how much money you're making. You can look at costs and work out ways to reduce them. You can also see if you are likely to have cash flow problems, giving yourself time to do something about them.

When you've made a budget, you should stick to it as far as possible, but review and revise it as needed, monthly if possible.

"Manage your spending by creating and sticking to a budget."
- Alexa von Tabel

TIPS

- Make a start.

- Make time for budgeting — set aside enough time to be able to prepare a comprehensive and realistic budget. The time needed will depend on the complexity of your business but initially I would set aside a morning or afternoon.

- Use last year's figures as a guide — information on previous sales and costs will give you a good indication of likely sales and costs. But it's also essential to consider what your sales plans are and how these will impact on the figures.

- Create realistic budgets — don't overestimate income or underestimate costs.

- Monitor the key drivers of your business, such as sales, costs and working capital.

- Involve the right people — don't work on the budget in isolation; ask staff with financial responsibilities to provide you with estimates of figures for your budget, e.g. sales targets, production costs. In this way you will achieve a more realistic budget. Also, by involving them this will give them greater commitment to meeting the budget.

- If you are a sole trader or sole director you could talk to people in similar businesses and ask them for their tips. Or speak to your accountant, if you have one.

Review regularly

To use your budgets effectively, you will need to review and revise them frequently, monthly if possible. This is particularly true if your business is growing and you are planning to move into new area. You will need to undertake a full review every 12 months.

Using up to date budgets enables you to be flexible and also lets you manage your cash flow and identify what needs to be achieved in the next budgeting period.

Look at the most significant differences that arise between your budgeted and actual figures.

Two main areas to consider:

1. Your actual income — each month compare your actual income with your sales budget by:
- analysing the reasons for any shortfall — for example, lower sales volumes;
- considering the reasons for a particularly high turnover — for example, whether your targets were too low; and
- comparing the timing of your income with your projections and checking that they fit.

By looking at the differences between your budgeted income and actual income, this will help you to set future budgets more accurately and also allow you to take action where needed.

2. Your actual expenditure — regularly review your actual expenditure against your budgeted expenditure. This will help you to predict future costs with better reliability. You should:
- look at your actual costs compared with your budget;
- consider if costs have significantly increased because turnover has; and
- assess if the actual timing of payments agrees to your budget.

Budgets can be prepared using spreadsheets; a basic template is shown on the next page:

Budget

	April			May			June			July		
	Actual £	Budget £	Variance £	Actual £	Budget £	Variance £	Actual £	Budget £	Variance £	Actual £	Budget £	Variance £
Projected sales income												
Product 1		0			0			0			0	
Product 2		0			0			0			0	
Service 1		0			0			0			0	
Service 2		0			0			0			0	
	0	0	0	0	0	0	0	0	0	0	0	0
Expenditure												
Direct costs		0			0			0			0	
Carriage		0			0			0			0	
Wages		0			0			0			0	
Fixed costs		0			0			0			0	
Rent		0			0			0			0	
Council tax		0			0			0			0	
Utilities		0			0			0			0	
Staff costs		0			0			0			0	
Motor expenses		0			0			0			0	
Telephone		0			0			0			0	
Printing, postage & stationery		0			0			0			0	
PR & advertising		0			0			0			0	
Professional fees		0			0			0			0	
Accountancy		0			0			0			0	
Training		0			0			0			0	
Insurance		0			0			0			0	
Repairs & maintenance		0			0			0			0	
Bank charges		0			0			0			0	
Sundry expenses		0			0			0			0	
	0	0	0	0	0	0	0	0	0	0	0	0
Net Cash flow		0			0			0			0	
Opening balance		0			0			0			0	
Closing balance		0			0			0			0	

Alternatively, you could use accounting software. I've already mentioned Quick-Books and Xero in chapter 4 but another one is Freshbooks. These three are the most popular packages.

You need to carry out your own research so that you can decide what's right for you.

You need to look at:
- whether it is suitable for small to medium businesses.
- whether it is suitable for your industry.
- how easy the software is to use and learn.
- whether it has customizable reports.
- functionality to manage multiple users.
- whether it can cope with large amounts of transaction data.
- help & support.
- security.

Prices tend to vary and can be payable monthly or annually.

As ever, choose a system that you understand as you are more likely to keep it up to date.

If you are still unsure of the value of preparing a budget, here is what Doreen had to say about how it had an impact on her business:

"I never thought that preparing a budget was worth the time and effort. However, by working through the steps, it has given me much more focus on my business. I now review and update my budget on a monthly basis. Having the budget in place has saved me a lot of time and money as it has given me greater clarity."

In order to budget you need to make a start and this is always easier once you have a plan in place — and there's no time like the present!

MY ACTION PLAN FOR BUDGETING

	Action:
1. I will decide on the budget period:	12 months ☐ 24 months ☐ 36 months ☐
2. I will set aside 3 hours to gather <u>all</u> projected sales and costs on:	
3. I will decide on which type of system I'll use:	Spreadsheet ☐ Accounting software ☐
4. I will enter the sales and costs information on:	
5. I will review <u>all</u> costs to see if any can be reduced on:	
6. I will review and revise my budget:	Every week ☐ Every month ☐ Every quarter ☐

As I've said, a budget is an incredibly useful tool to help you achieve your business goals. Good luck with preparing yours, but remember:

> *"A budget tells us what we can't afford, but it doesn't keep us from buying it."*
> *- William Feather*

CHAPTER 8

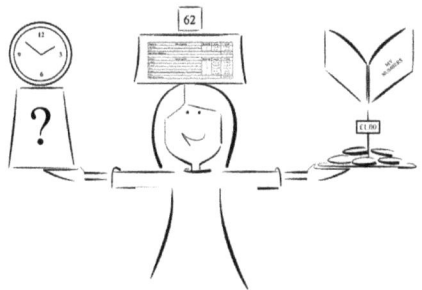

MANAGING YOUR BUSINESS

"Management is all about managing in the short term, while developing the plans for the future."
- Jack Welch

Management accounts are a planning tool for your business and are essential to help you do it your way. They will help you decide which areas of your business you need to focus on.

"A clear vision, backed by definite plans, gives you a tremendous feeling of confidence and personal power."
- Brian Tracy, The Gift of Self-Confidence

You need a plan otherwise your business will lack direction. You need to keep a regular eye on the company's figures otherwise you may not recognise that your pricing is too high or that your profits are lower than you thought even though turnover is high.

Information needs to be **timely** — basing your decision on end of year accounts is too late as you aren't in a situation where you are predicting what to do next but in fact fire-fighting a situation which has occurred.

Information needs to be the correct **regularity** for you and your business — this can be monthly, quarterly, 6-monthly, or whatever suits you, but at least 6-monthly and means you are keeping an accurate eye on what's going on now and what you need to do.

Management accounts are basically a profit and loss account and balance sheet (more information in chapter 5) at a particular point in time. The budgeted figures from the previous period are compared with the actual figures and any variances (differences) are investigated.

PROFIT AND LOSS ACCOUNT COMPARISON
FROM MAY 2018 TO JUNE 2018

	Month Jun-18 £	Month May-18 £	Variance £
SALES	230,922	172,452	58,470
Vehicle costs	66,829	57,958	(8,871)
Wages and national insurance	69,106	63,614	(5,492)
Sub-contract costs	9,334	11,167	1,833
Depreciation	5,606	5,606	0
Cost of sales	150,875	138,345	(12,530)
Gross profit	80,047	34,107	45,940
OVERHEADS			
Rent, rates, water and utilities	11,912	12,040	128
Repairs and maintenance	1,000	1,289	289
Wages and salaries	18,971	15,203	(3,768)
Pension	505	505	0
Telephone	2,231	1,335	(896)
Printing, postage and stationery	693	1,484	791
Insurance	238	368	130
Sundry expenses	124	0	(124)
Bank charges	129	133	4
Accountancy fees	3,550	438	(3,112)
Legal fees	1,501	0	(1,501)
Depreciation	276	275	(1)
	41,130	33,070	(8,060)
Net profit (loss)	38,917	1,037	37,880

YOUR BUSINESS YOUR NUMBERS

MANAGEMENT ACCOUNTS
FOR THE PERIOD ENDING: 31/01/2018

BALANCE SHEET	Last year end	As at month end	Year end forecast
	£000	£000	£000
Fixed assets	21,523	22,241	26,937
Current assets			
Trade debtors	176	110	150
Other current assets	396	302	300
Cash and short-term investments	2,705	2,924	2,490
	3,277	3,336	2,940
Current liabilities			
Trade creditors	180	184	200
Accrued expenses	1,089	1,340	1,300
Loans	55	57	315
Other payables	834	849	900
	2,158	2,430	2,715
Net current assets	1,119	906	225
Long term liabilities			
Provisions	470	413	225
Loans	7,574	7,550	12,359
	8,044	7,963	12,584
Net Assets Employed	14,598	15,184	14,578
Capital and reserves			
Called up share capital	100	100	100
Profit and loss account	14,498	15,084	14,478
Total Funds	14,598	15,184	14,578

Management accounts can be prepared using software or spreadsheets. If you're asking your accountant to prepare them, make sure he/she knows what the important figures are that you need highlighting, e.g. labour costs, net profit, advertising, corporation tax. Which numbers are important will depend on your particular business; for example, the ones to highlight will be labour and fuel for a transport company. But for a catering company, this will be labour and raw material costs.

How management accounts will help you to achieve your goals:
- By planning
- By preparation
- By encouraging you to be more forward thinking
- By helping you to see the next step you need to take to reach your goals.

Management accounts are useful for a business as they:
- give a summary of significant figures,
- highlight differences between actual and budgeted figures, and
- focus your mind on moving your business forward.

I'd suggest working through the action plan at the end of the chapter to see how management accounts could help your business.

Maintaining management accounts will help you to know when you reach the turnover figure that means you need to be VAT registered.

Apologies, but there is a lot to take in with the next section. However, I believe it's important to have a knowledge of how VAT works even though you may not be at the VAT limit yet. So here we go!

WHY BECOME VAT REGISTERED?

Value Added Tax (VAT) is charged on the majority of goods and services provided by VAT registered businesses in the UK, as well as certain goods and services that are imported from non-EU countries and those imported into the UK from other EU countries.

VAT registration is a voluntary measure for any small business with a taxable turnover of less than £85,000 for the previous 12 months of trading, but above £85,000 it is mandatory.

ADVANTAGES OF BECOMING VAT REGISTERED (WHETHER VOLUNTARY OR LEGALLY REQUIRED)

- VAT can then be reclaimed on most goods or services that are purchased by the business.

- It can give the appearance that your business is bigger than it actually is. So if you are trying to give the impression that your business is a large established one, then becoming VAT registered will benefit you.

DISADVANTAGES OF BECOMING VAT REGISTERED

- You suddenly make your goods and services 20% more expensive to customers who aren't VAT registered.

- You could end up with a large VAT bill from HMRC if your business has generated more VAT from goods and services sold than VAT paid on goods and services purchased.

- It adds to the admin side of your business. You have to keep records of all VAT invoices and receipts, maintain accounting records and submit a return every three months.

VAT SCHEMES

When registering for VAT, think about when you want your VAT quarters to end. It is always easier for your accountant if your year-end date is the same as the end of a VAT quarter.

There are several VAT schemes to choose from and it is important to choose the right one for your business:
- Standard VAT
- Cash Accounting Scheme
- Flat Rate Scheme
- Annual Accounting Scheme

All schemes except for the annual accounting scheme require quarterly returns to be made.

Standard VAT Accounting

Any VAT due to HMRC or owed back to you is payable quarterly. You pay VAT on your sales and reclaim VAT on your purchases, regardless of whether the invoices have been paid. The amount of VAT due to HMRC is the difference between the VAT charged to your customers and the VAT on your purchases.

There are no restrictions on eligibility for the standard VAT accounting scheme. You must use this scheme if:
- you issue VAT invoices with payment terms of six months or more, or raise VAT invoices in advance;
- you buy or sell goods through lease or hire purchase or conditional sale; or
- you import goods from within the EU.

Example:

	Net value	VAT	Total
Sales invoices	10,000	2,000	12,000
Purchases	5,000	1,000	6,000
VAT due to HMRC		1,000	

(VAT on sales invoices less VAT on purchase invoices)

Cash Accounting Scheme

With the cash accounting scheme, you only pay VAT when your customers pay you, and only reclaim VAT on your purchases when you have paid your suppliers. This scheme may be useful if your customers take a long time to pay you.

To join the scheme your annual taxable turnover must be less than £1.35m.

Example:

	Net value	VAT	Total
Sales invoices raised	10,000	2,000	12,000
Purchase invoices received	5,000	1,000	6,000
Sales invoices paid	6,000	1,200	7,200
Purchase invoices paid	4,000	800	4,800
VAT due to HMRC		400	

(VAT on sales less VAT on purchases)

Flat Rate Scheme

With the Flat Rate Scheme you pay a fixed rate of VAT to HMRC. You cannot reclaim VAT on your purchases, unless they are for certain capital items over £2,000.

Previously this scheme was especially attractive to service businesses with a small amount of purchase VAT. But from April 2017 onwards, HMRC introduced a new ruling and if you are classed as a limited cost trader you have to pay flat rate VAT at 16.5% so overall it is no longer a good idea to use flat rate compared with standard. You're classed as a limited cost trader if your goods cost less than either:
- 2% of your turnover
- £1,000 a year (if your costs are more than 2%)

To join the scheme your annual taxable turnover must be £150,000 or less and you must apply to HMRC. The rate of VAT you pay depends on the type of business you run and is applied to your 'flat rate turnover'. You can find out the relevant rate from the HMRC website; rates vary between businesses:

Catering services including restaurants and takeaways	12.5
General building or construction services	9.5
Manufacturing food	9

This is different to the turnover used in the standard VAT accounting scheme.

Example:

You bill a customer for £1,000, adding VAT at 20% to make £1,200 in total.

You're a caterer, so the VAT flat rate for your business is 12.5%.

Your flat rate payment will be 12.5% of £1,200 (or £150).

Annual Accounting Scheme

With the annual accounting scheme you submit one VAT return a year, and make advance payments towards the VAT bill based on your previous bill. When you submit your return you either make a final payment to make up the shortfall, or apply for a refund if you have paid too much.

If you regularly reclaim VAT this scheme would not be suitable because you would only get one refund a year.

You can join the scheme if your annual taxable turnover is less than £1.35m.

Once You Are Registered

You must keep accurate records of sales and purchases. If you have a significant number of transactions it is worth investing in a computerised accounting system. HMRC can visit your business to inspect your record keeping and charge you a penalty if your records aren't in order. You must keep your records for at least six years.

You should ensure that each sales invoice has a unique number. You should also quote your VAT number on each invoice.

You must keep copies of your VAT returns and the proof for each one. You will need these in the event of an inspection.

Always ask for VAT receipts for any purchases that you are reclaiming VAT on. Some businesses may not be VAT registered and you cannot reclaim VAT on these purchases.

You cannot reclaim any VAT on entertainment expenses, and there are special rules for working how much VAT to reclaim on motor expenses and staff travel expenses. For more information, go to the HMRC website.

Some items are outside the scope of VAT, such as staff wages and payments to HMRC for Pay as You Earn (PAYE), National Insurance Contributions (NIC), Corporation Tax and VAT. These should not be included in your VAT return. Other items that should be excluded include road tax, MOT costs, rates, loan repayments, drawings and dividends paid.

If you choose to use spreadsheets to keep you records it is worth considering using the example on the next page as a template:

Income

Date	Customer	Total	VAT	Sales	Interest
01/01/2016	Smith & Co	1,200.00	200.00	1,000.00	
31/01/2016	Bank Plc	10.00			10.00
05/02/2016	Browns Ltd	1,800.00	300.00	1,500.00	
29/02/2016	Bank Plc	15.00			15.00
03/03/2016	Green Plc	3,600.00	600.00	3,000.00	
31/03/2016	Bank Plc	20.00			20.00
		6,645.00	1,100.00	5,500.00	45.00
			Box 1	Box 6	Box 6

Purchases

Date	Details	Total	VAT	Wages	Post	Stationery	Rent
15/01/2016	Rent	1,200.00	200.00				1,000.00
20/02/2016	Post Office	1.60			1.60		
29/02/2016	Wages	2,000.00		2,000.00			
05/03/2016	Paper	1.20	0.20			1.00	
14/03/2016	Rent	1,200.00	200.00				1,000.00
		4,402.80	400.20	2,000.00	1.60	1.00	2,000.00
			Box 4	Box 7	Box 7	Box 7	Box 7

VAT return

VAT due this period on sales and other outputs	1	1,100.00
VAT due this period on acquisitions from other EC Member States	2	-
Total VAT due (the sum of boxes 1 and 2)	3	1,100.00
VAT reclaimed in the period on purchases and other inputs (including acquisitions from the EC)	4	400.20
VAT to Pay Customs	5	**699.80**

Sales and Purchases Excluding VAT

Total value of sales and all other outputs excluding VAT (include your box 8 figure)	6	5,545.00
Total value of purchases and all other inputs excluding VAT (include your box 9 figure)	7	2,002.60

EC Supplies and Purchases Excluding VAT

Total value of all supplies of goods, excluding and VAT, to other EC Member States	8	-
Total value of all acquisitions of goods, excluding any VAT, from other EC Member States	9	-

If you import goods from non-EU countries and use an agent to deal with the declarations and import duty and VAT payments, you will receive a form C79 each month. This form shows the import VAT paid that month which should be included on your VAT return. You must keep these forms as they are the proof for your VAT reclaim.

Moving goods between EU countries is much simpler and the VAT return form has specific boxes for recording the sales and purchases figures.

EXIT PLANNING

It's easy to concentrate on spending your time helping your business to run smoothly. Of course, this is essential as it's your livelihood, but it's also crucial to think long term.

Peter Gray, Partner at Cavendish, a consultancy that helps businesses to find buyers, states that exit planning needs to be thought about 3 to 5 years prior to selling a business.

Maybe take some time to think about it now, answering the following questions:
1. When would you like to retire?
2. Do you want to retire in one move or plan ahead and do it in a specific amount of years?
3. Do you want to ease yourself out of the business over a few years?
4. Are you emotionally ready to let go of your business?
5. What will happen to your business when you retire?
6. Will you sell your business to an outside buyer or will it be passed to your family/children?
7. What do you plan to do when you retire?

If you are thinking of passing your business on to your family, then you need to consider whether this is the correct course of action.
- Is this something you would like to happen but you haven't asked your family/children?
- Is this what they want to do with their life?
- Are they interested in your business?
- Do they have the necessary skills?

As Elizabeth Bagger, Executive Director of the Institute for Family Businesses states:

> *"The process must always be about answering questions like "what are we in business for?" and "what must we do to achieve our plans?" Framing it like this forces owners to assess the skills they have or don't have, and who might need to come onboard. Only then is the emotion removed, and bosses can look at other solutions like employee-ownership, new management, buyouts or the family taking a side role on a family board."*

Effective exit planning needs to start early and take into account a whole range of issues in order to maximise the value of the business when you sell.

What can you do now to get ready:

- Timing — What will be the right stage in the business lifecycle to get the most interest from potential purchasers?

- Get organized — Make sure all your paperwork and records are tidy and easily accessible.

- Systems — Are management systems, legal agreements and so on robust?

- Tax — What will be the most tax-efficient way to extract money from the business?

- Premises — How are they looking? Do they need to be spruced up?

- Adding value — Is there anything it would be worth doing now to add value? for example, getting planning permission for future expansion

- Your current role in the business — At the moment, do you have holidays? Who covers for you when you are away? Do you need to start delegating more of your duties and give your staff more responsibility? It's a good time now to start reducing your day-to-day involvement with the business.

Please use the table on the next page to start your exit planning.

PREPARING YOUR EXIT STRATEGY

	Review on (date)	Action (✓)
1. When will be the right stage of the business cycle to stop?		
2. Are all your paperwork and records filed?		
3. Are all your legal and management systems set up correctly?		
4. What will be the most tax-efficient way to get money out of your business?		
5. Do you need to update your premises?		
6. Is there anything you need to put in place to add value to your business?		
7. Any changes you need to make in the way you work so that the business can continue successfully without you?		

If you put all of these in place, then you can be confident that your business will continue to thrive. Don't start slowing down yet; in order to make your business attractive you need to work harder.

There are many areas to think of when managing your business and making it successful — from using management accounts, to VAT registration, to thinking of your exit strategy. Lots to think about as always! There is a table to complete on the next page that will help you use management accounts for your business.

MANAGEMENT ACCOUNTS ACTION PLAN

	Action
1. Using management accounts will help me to: • Save time • Plan • Set strategies to achieve my goals *Prioritise in order of importance* *(1 being most useful)*	✓ ☐ ☐ ☐
2. I will start using management accounts from:	
3. Management accounts will be prepared:	Monthly/quarterly/half yearly *(Delete as appropriate)*
4. They will be prepared by:	Me/my bookkeeper/my accountant *(Delete as appropriate)*
5. The numbers to highlight are: • Turnover • Gross profit • Net profit • Labour costs • Advertising • Corporation tax • Other	✓ ☐ ☐ ☐ ☐ ☐ ☐ ☐
6. I will review my management accounts compared with my budget each month/quarter/half year, starting on:	
7. I will investigate all variances (differences) between the actual figures compared with the budgeted ones:	

CHAPTER 9

MASTERING YOUR PERSONAL FINANCES

"The most important factor to growing your financial stability isn't your income. Rather, your success is much more related to how well you keep your eye on the ball. Organize your finances around the principles of financial stability. Aim for that goal, and over time you will find many unexpected ways to actually put money aside."
- Erik Wecks, How to Manage Your Money When You Don't Have Any

How you manage, spend and invest your money can have a profound impact on your life. I know when you work for yourself, frequently you don't manage your personal finances as well as your business finances — you're too busy working on your business! But you need to do it and do it in the way that suits you.

Going through school we're taught maths, but many people never learn basic money management. Skills like creating a budget, investing for the future, or even how credit cards work are thin on the ground. I have already talked about budgeting for business in chapter 7 but your personal finances are equally important. Of course, many of the same principles apply.

THE BASICS OF PERSONAL FINANCE

Managing your finances feels like nothing but a lot of paperwork and numbers. You make X amount, you spend Y amount, and you try to make sure Y is less than X. However, your finances are just as much about psychology, habits, and the values you choose to live by. Your mindset is so important! That's why I keep saying do it your way!

> *"You don't have to be a miser, just be wiser with your money."*
> - Dorethia Conner Kelly, #MoneyChat THE BOOK: How To Get Out of Debt, Successfully Manage Your Money and Create Financial Security!

There are a few rules that will always help improve your financial life:

1. Spend less than you earn: If you earn £40,000 per year and you spend £41,000 per year, you'll be in a debt position that's hard to get out of. If you spend exactly as much as you earn every year, you'll never have money in the bank for emergencies. Spending less than you earn means you can save, prepare for the future, and deal with any emergencies too. It will give you a comfort blanket!

2. Always plan: This doesn't just mean retirement, although having a retirement plan will ensure you have an income when you're unable to work anymore. Establishing an emergency fund will allow you to deal with unexpected car or home repairs. Your finances should always look forward beyond the current month. Then if something unexpected happens you will be ready for it!

3. Invest your money: Properly invested money earns more money over time. Don't just put all your cash away in a low-interest savings account. Invest in things that will earn you more money than you had before, such as shares. This doesn't have to be complicated and if you need help then ask!

SET GOALS

But where do you start? Sometimes it can seem a bit overwhelming, can't it? Think about what you want from your life and set some goals.

In the same way you set SMART goals for your business in chapter 2, think about setting personal goals which are specific.

Break your goals down into actions so that they are more achievable.

Maybe you have a goal to:
- travel the world,
- retire early,
- own a home,
- start a family, or
- move or change career.

You are more likely to achieve your goals if you manage your finances well. If you are in a debt position, it may seem impossible to consider goals such as this, but think about what you really want to do. We will tackle the steps to overcome debt in a bit.

Once you have written down your goals you will need to prioritize them. This makes sure you are paying attention to the ones that are most important to you. And you're less likely to get distracted!

Start by setting long-term goals like getting out of debt, buying a home, or retiring early. One of my clients has always planned to retire at 55 and therefore decided years ago that he would start investing in property to enable him to retire and live off the rental income. Another decided many years ago that after working in the civil service all of his life he wanted to be self-employed, working as an organ repairer when he retired. And he has done it very successfully! Having these long-term goals can help you focus on your shorter-term goals.

Getting out of debt has to be the priority. It is important to prioritise the order of what you do, for example, move a high interest credit card to a 0% one and agree to pay a certain amount each month, then reduce spending, manage bills and look for best deals on energy etc. Obviously, if you can increase your income as you go then even better!

Then set short-term goals, like following a budget, decreasing your spending, or stop using your credit cards.

CREATE A PLAN

A plan will help you reach your goals and should start with these:

- Get control of your budget.
- Get out of debt.

After you have accomplished those two things, you should decide what you want to do with your money to reach your goals. The money you free up from your debt payments can be used to reach your goals. At this point, you should decide which priorities are the most important to you right now. As long as you are steadily working towards your long-term retirement goals, you can begin to focus on the most important goals you have set for yourself. Your goals, along with an emergency fund, will help you stop making financial decisions based on fear and help you get control of your situation. Think how fantastic that will make you feel!

To achieve your goals and stick to your plan remember:
- Your budget is key to success. It is the tool that will give you the most control of your financial future. Your budget can help you achieve the rest of your plan.
- Use budgeting software or past expenses to get you a starting point for your budget.
- Take the time to focus on your budget now.

HOW TO SET UP A BUDGET

The first step to taking control of your finances is creating a budget.

> *"Budgeting has only one rule: Do not go over budget."*
> - Leslie Tayne, *Life & Debt: A Fresh Approach to Achieving Financial Wellness*

It will take a little effort, but it's a great way to get a quick snapshot of the money you have coming in and going out.

Setting up a budget means you're:
- less likely to end up in debt;
- less likely to get caught out by unexpected costs;
- more likely to have a good credit rating;
- more likely to be accepted for a mortgage or loan;
- able to spot areas where you can make savings; and
- in a great position to save up for a holiday, a new car, or another treat.

Over half of UK households keep a regular budget. Most say it gives them peace of mind about how much they are spending and makes them feel better about life in general.

To get started on your budget, you'll need to work out how much you spend on:
- household bills,
- living costs,
- financial products (insurance etc.),
- family and friends (presents etc.),
- travel (car costs, public transport etc.), and
- leisure (holidays, sport, restaurants, hairdressers etc.)

Just grab as much information as you can about your income and spending (bills, bank statements etc.) and get started. If you don't keep these items in one place, it's worth starting now. Remember to include all of the costs that you pay out monthly: don't forget TV licences, maintenance costs etc.

Budgets can be prepared using spreadsheets; a basic template is shown below

CASH BUDGET													
NAME:													
YEAR END:													
RECEIPTS	Jan	Feb	Mar	April	May	June	July	Aug	Sept	Oct	Nov	Dec	Total
Salary													0.00
Self-employed income													0.00
TOTAL RECEIPTS	0.00	0.00	0.00	0.00	0.00	0.00	0.00	0.00	0.00	0.00	0.00	0.00	0.00
PAYMENTS	Jan	Feb	Mar	April	May	June	July	Aug	Sept	Oct	Nov	Dec	Total
Mortgage													0.00
Council tax													0.00
Utilities													0.00
Insurance													0.00
Groceries													0.00
Vehicle costs													0.00
Subscriptions													0.00
Travel													0.00
Sundries													0.00
TOTAL PAYMENTS	0.00	0.00	0.00	0.00	0.00	0.00	0.00	0.00	0.00	0.00	0.00	0.00	0.00
Net cash flow	0.00	0.00	0.00	0.00	0.00	0.00	0.00	0.00	0.00	0.00	0.00	0.00	0.00
Opening balance @		0.00	0.00	0.00	0.00	0.00	0.00	0.00	0.00	0.00	0.00	0.00	
Closing balance	0.00	0.00	0.00	0.00	0.00	0.00	0.00	0.00	0.00	0.00	0.00	0.00	

There are also some great free budgeting apps available and your bank or building society might have an online budgeting tool that takes information directly from your transactions.

GETTING YOUR BUDGET BACK ON TRACK

Do you know where your money goes or does it just disappear?

Start by calculating how much money you earn each month.

If you're spending more than you have coming in, you need to work out where you can cut back — sometimes ruthlessly! This could be as easy as making your lunch at home, cancelling a gym membership you don't use or cutting down on coffees. You could also keep a spending diary and keep a note of everything you buy in a month. It's quite surprising, when you write everything down, to discover how much you spend. Or, if you do most of your spending with a bank card, look at last month's bank statement and work out where your money is going.

GET EVERYONE INVOLVED

Get everyone in your family involved in keeping to a budget. Sit down together and make a plan that you can all stick to.

Work out how much spending money is available and agree between you what you'll each have.

CUTTING YOUR HOUSEHOLD BILLS AND YOUR MORTGAGE

Household bills make up a large chunk of your spending so it's important to take control of them. A good way of doing this is to review the utility and phone payment amounts regularly, say every year.

You can also save hundreds and even thousands of pounds by shopping around for a new mortgage, or reviewing the one you already have. I know this is one of those jobs that tends to be put off but I know from experience it can make a massive difference. Just do it!

BE FLEXIBLE

Life is unpredictable so try to review your budget and your spending if there's a change, or at least every couple of months. For example, one of my clients had to take 6 months off work to care for his stepson when he was seriously ill. Another client became ill himself and went from working long hours to having to work part time. We never know what is around the corner, so if things change then make sure you update your budget.

You might get a pay rise, which means you can save more, or you might find your household bills increase.

Once you get the hang of tracking your expenses, you can try using a service like Mint to manage it for you https://www.mint.co.uk/

Connect your bank account and it will automatically tag your transactions, so you can easily see how much you're spending on bills, groceries, restaurants, shopping, and other categories. You can also use it to set budgets for different things like groceries or entertainment and get notified when you're going over.

STICK TO YOUR BUDGET

Even after you are out of debt you need to have a budget. It is easy to spend more than you make, and if you stop tracking your spending you can go over and run up debt really quickly. A budget helps you decide how to spend your money. Without the plan, you may spend your money on things that are not important to you, and then wonder why you never hit your goals.

GET OUT OF DEBT

Often, the hardest part of paying off your debts is making a start. It's easy to feel overwhelmed if you know you're struggling financially. It's tempting to bury your head in the sand and ignore your bank statements and demands for payment, but it won't make the problem any better and could make it worse.

So, take a deep breath and open any letters you've been ignoring — this isn't going to go away! Once you've done this, at least you'll know what you have to deal with and you can work out what you need to do next.

Your debt is a huge obstacle to reaching your financial goals, so make a plan to clear your debts. While making minimum payments, focus extra money on one debt at a time and then move all the money you were paying on the first debt to the next debt. Once you are out of debt, you need to make a commitment to stay out of debt. Stop carrying your credit cards around with you and save up an emergency fund to cover unexpected expenses so you do not need to turn to a credit card to cover them.

- Maybe you have items you can sell on eBay to give you extra cash.
- A second job can help to clear debts.
- Look for expenditure you can cut in your budget to increase your debt payments too.

PAYING OFF LOANS AND CREDIT CARDS

If you have loans or owe money on credit cards it usually makes sense to pay off the debt that charges the highest rate of interest first.

Examples include:
- Credit cards;
- Store cards, which normally charge the highest rates of interest; and
- Personal loans from the bank, which normally charge a lower rate of interest than credit or store cards.

It is important to make sure you don't break the terms of your agreements.

So even if you're focusing on paying off another debt, you must pay at least the minimum on any credit cards and your monthly required payments on any loan agreements.

HOW TO USE CREDIT CARDS WITHOUT GOING INTO DEBT

Despite how easy it is to get a credit card, it's also easy to get overwhelmed and wind up owing too much money. However, credit cards can also be really useful — when used correctly. Remember: don't use a credit card to buy things you couldn't otherwise afford. Instead, only buy something if you have the money in your account right now, and pay off your card's balance every month.

If you only pay the minimum amount due, most of your payment will go towards interest. This means your balance will remain high and keep generating interest. Even if you can't afford to pay off the whole balance in one month, at least pay more than the minimum.

So if you're only supposed to pay for what you can afford, then what's the point of having a credit card instead of a debit card? Well, when used properly, there are a few key benefits:

- **You can earn rewards**: Most credit cards come with different kinds of rewards based on how much you spend. It could be cash back, it could be airline miles, hotel points, or even Amazon gift cards.

- **You're protected against fraud**: Sometimes, a bank will offer to refund debit card purchases, but for the most part, they're treated the same as cash. Credit cards, on the other hand, are completely protected.

- **You can get protection for all kinds of purchases**: Many cards will offer extended warranties on bigger items such as TVs, damage protection on your mobile if you pay your monthly bill with your credit card, or travel insurance on a flight you paid for with your card.

Credit cards can be incredibly useful tools for a properly planned budget, but they can also be destructive if you don't use them carefully. So, think about the kind of person you are and, if they aren't necessary, don't use them.

GETTING HELP IF DEBT PROBLEMS BECOME SERIOUS

If you've already missed credit card or loan payments or if you're behind with rent, mortgage etc. then take advice from a free debt advice charity straight away. Here are some links which you may find useful:
- www.advice-debts.com
- www.national-debt-help.com/Government/Legislation

INVESTING YOUR SAVINGS

So, you've started budgeting your money, you're building credit, and you're spending less than you earn. Maybe it took you a couple months, but you're finally in control of your finances. Great! Now comes the next part: saving for the future.

Maybe you haven't thought much about the future. Maybe it seems too far away to matter, or maybe it feels impossible and overwhelming. However, the earlier you start saving, the more money you'll have later on in life — and the less effort you'll spend trying to get there later on.

> *"If you're saving, you're succeeding."*
> *- Steve Burkholder*

Once you are ready to grow your wealth and begin investing you should speak to a Financial Planner to help you make your investment decisions. A good advisor will share the risks involved in each investment, and help you find products that match your risk level while helping you work towards your goals as quickly as possible. They will help you to make an investment plan based on your goals and timeframes.

Remember that investing is a long-term strategy to building wealth and as I said earlier, it doesn't have to be complicated.

SET A SAVINGS GOAL

Some people find it hard to get motivated about saving, but it's often much easier if you set a goal.

Your first step is to have some emergency savings — money to fall back on if you have an emergency, such as a boiler breakdown, or if you can't work for a while.

Try to get three months' worth of expenses in an easy or instant access account. This may take a while to build up but have it as a target.

The best way to save money is to pay some money into a savings account every month. Initially, this may only be a small amount but it will make you feel better that you're taking control.

INVESTING

Investing doesn't have to be complicated, but it's worth getting advice. A Financial Planner will work through the process of setting up an investment plan with you based on your age, goals, and risk preferences.

Getting started with long-term investments will often be one of the hardest parts of your financial life because, when you're just starting out, you don't have much money. For that reason, it's important that you re-examine your investments every time you get a raise or a new job that pays you more. When you make more money, it's tempting to upgrade your life with say a new car to match your new budget. Tempting though this is, remember you'll never have a better time to boost your long-term savings than when you're already living on a smaller budget than you're earning.

Getting to grips with your personal finances isn't easy but it is very satisfying and uplifting when you get there. Having control of your personal finances will have a knock-on impact on your business; you will be under less stress, waste less time and therefore you will be able to concentrate on improving your business.

If you are a sole trader it is even more important to sort out your personal finances as the line between you personally and the business is less clear.

You may find this software useful to keep on top of your finances:

> http://www.banktree.co.uk/

Good luck with taking control of your finances.

PERFECT PERSONAL FINANCE — SETTING YOUR GOALS

Taking control of your personal finances and getting a financial life plan in place will help you feel more secure and in control.

This book is a great help when you set your own financial life plan: *Dream it, Plan it, Live It* by Karl Lehmann.

You have already set your business goals — now it's time to set your own goals! This could be that you want to clear your credit card in the next 6 months. In the same way as you need to run your business in your way, it's important to take control of your personal finances in your own way too. It's amazing how empowering that can be!

Write down 3 goals you want to achieve in the next 3 months. Alongside each goal, write down an action. Make sure you decide when you are going to start and complete each action and, most importantly, how are you going to celebrate completing the action! Maybe not going out on a wild shopping spree, but you could go to the cinema, theatre or have a meal.

\	SHORT-TERM GOALS (Next 3 months)		
Goals	Action(s)	Date	Celebration
1.			
2.			
3.			

\	LONG-TERM GOALS (12 months and over)		
Goals	Action(s)	Date	Celebration
1.			
2.			
3.			

OVER TO YOU

"Authenticity is everything! You have to wake up every day and look in the mirror, and you want to be proud of the person who's looking back at you. And you can only do that if you're being honest with yourself and being a person of high character. You have an opportunity every single day to write that story of your life."
—Aaron Rodgers

We spend so much of our time immersed in our business, it's crucial to work in an authentic way so that the way we are in and outside of our business is aligned. By being true to yourself you will find that running your business is easier as you're not fighting against yourself.

All that remains is for me to wish you all the best and please keep in touch with me. Remember to shout out about your successes!

> **Here are my details:**
>
> *Facebook* ▸ facebook.com/agoodwinaccountancy
>
> *Twitter* ▸ @AccountantAnna
>
> *LinkedIn* ▸ linkedin.com/in/annagoodwinaccountancy

Good Luck!

Anna

*Today you are YOU,
that is TRUER than true.
There is NO ONE alive
who is YOUER than YOU!*
  -Dr Seuss

ACKNOWLEDGEMENTS

Thanks to:

Sian-Elin Flint-Freel for all of her help and time in proof reading and editing. All of the Skype calls were invaluable in helping me to keep motivated and moving forward. Meeting up in Buxton for a face to face brainstorming session was the icing on the cake!

Rachel Robb of Rachel Robb content writer and marketer for all her advice and tips and helping me to review the illustrations and chapter titles.

Nicola Kucharski for typing the book and entering tables.

Lucy Monkman for all the wonderful illustrations and book cover!

Tanya Back for her typesetting skills.

Sarah Wood for keeping me motivated and being there at the end of the week for a few drinks to rejuvenate ready to start again.

Diane Cleary for being there to chat through and brainstorm issues with the book and illustrations – fun and useful sessions!

To all the reviewers for your lovely comments and sparing your time to read this book.

To all my staff who kept the accountancy work flowing.

To friends and family for being supportive.

Last but not least, Neil Gooding, for his ongoing support while I have been engrossed in writing this book.

Lightning Source UK Ltd.
Milton Keynes UK
UKHW02f2228150918
328970UK00004B/11/P